THE
WALKING BREAD

The Bread Will Rise

a cookbook (and a parody)

by Hallee Bridgeman

a.k.a. "Hallee the Homemaker™"

BRINGING NEW LIFE TO OLD GRAIN

Published by

House of Bread Bo

HOUSE OF BREAD™

COPYRIGHT NOTICE

The Walking Bread, the bread will rise

Some scripture quotations courtesy of the King James Version of the Holy Bible.

Some scripture quotations courtesy of the New King James Version of the Holy Bible, Copyright © 1979, 1980, 1982 by Thomas-Nelson, Inc. Used by permission. All rights reserved.

Cover Art by Debi Warford (www.debiwarford.com)

PUBLISHED BY: House of Bread Books™*, an imprint of Olivia Kimbrell Press™, P.O. Box 4393, Winchester, KY 40392-4393

The House of Bread Books™ colophon and logo are trademarks of Olivia Kimbrell Press™.

*Olivia Kimbrell Press™ is a publisher offering true to life, meaningful fiction and relevant nonfiction from a Christian worldview intended to uplift the heart and engage the mind. For more information about the mission of House of Bread Books™, refer to our mission statement at the back of this book.

Library Cataloging Data
Bridgeman, Hallee (Hallee A. Bridgeman) 1972-
  The Walking Bread, the bread will rise/ Hallee Bridgeman
    150 p. 23cm x 15cm (9in x 6 in.)
Summary: Book 1 in Hallee's Galley parody cookbook series tangles with the cultural obsession with zombies while serving up delicious recipes.
 ISBN: 978-1-939603-31-9 (trade perfect) ISBN-10: 1-939603-31-5
 ISBN: 978-1-939603-09-8 (ebook)
1. real food 2. whole food 3. artisan cooking 4. natural living 5. parody 6. satire 7. recipes
 [Non-Fic.] 613-DC22

THE WALKING BREAD

The Bread Will Rise

a cookbook (and a parody)

by Hallee Bridgeman

a.k.a. "Hallee the Homemaker™"

Hallee's Galley book 2

EVIEWS

Submitted for your ultimate *breadification*, a cookbook that *rises* above the rest. Bake up a storm and consider the *proof* of a truth so powerful it once woke the dead.

Rave Reviews for The Walking Bread:

"I was in a *loaf* or death situation *yeast*erday, then I found this cookbook! Now I'm on a *roll*."
A homemaker in the **USA TODAY** said

"I used to rack my *grain* for hours trying to bake. I made such great bread with this book, my husband brought me *flours*."
THE TIMES this has been said are numerous

"If you *knead* to get serious about the zombie apocalypse, this cookbook is ammunition."
We're sure the **DAILY MIRROR** wishes they had quoted this

"Instead of *loafing* around, I learned how to bake! Now I don't feel so *crumby*!"
Part of **SOUTHERN LIVING** is overhearing these kinds of remarks now and then

"*Muffin* wrong with this cookbook. If you're serious about saving some *dough*, you *butter* memorize it. It's the *yeast* you can do."
A reader in **WEST VIRGINIA JOURNAL**ed

TABLE OF CONTENTS

FOREWORD

For years now I have been preparing recipes for the Hallee the Homemaker blog with the intent of publishing a cookbook. In all those years of preparing myself, until very recently, I never imagined that my first cookbook would be about GRAVY or that in writing my second cookbook, I would find myself parodying the flesh eating ZOMBIE fad. Seriously, who equates the undead with life-giving bread?

After writing *Fifty Shades of Gravy; A Christian Gets Saucy!*, I developed my writing mission statement: To prayerfully craft stories as modern day parables to uplift fellow believers and minister to seekers in our fallen world.

The Bible constantly and continuously references bread as a nourishment, as a gift from God, as life sustaining.

> "And wine that maketh glad the heart of man, and oil to make his face to shine, and **bread** which strengtheneth man's heart." Psalms 104:15

> "And your threshing shall reach unto the vintage, and the vintage shall reach unto the sowing time: and ye shall eat your **bread** to the full, and dwell in your land safely." Leviticus 26:5

As long as God's chosen people had bread, they survived. In times of famine, it was grain they sought, grain to make bread that would sustain physical life. It was even considered a worthy sacrifice to God:

> "Then it shall be, that, when ye eat of the **bread** of the land, ye shall offer up an heave offering unto the LORD. Ye shall offer up a cake of the first of your dough for an heave offering: as ye do the heave offering of the threshing floor, so shall ye heave it." Numbers 15:19-20

When Christ spoke of Himself, he referred to Himself as The Bread of Life.

> "For the **bread** of God is he which cometh down from heaven, and giveth life unto the world. Then said they unto him, Lord, evermore give us this bread. And Jesus said unto them, I am the bread of life: he that cometh to me shall never hunger; and he that believeth on me shall never thirst." John 6:33-35

Much like bread feeds our body, a relationship with our Lord Jesus Christ is what feeds our soul (see the "Invitation" in the back of this book). Much like Christ with his parables and sarcasm, I'm presenting this information to you in the form of a parody of a popular cultural phenomenon. I pray that you have fun with this book, that it gives you some tools and insight, and that you create amazing breads for your family and friends.

INTRODUCTION

Bread is an integral part of my family's daily diet. Because we use fresh ground grains, we get the full benefit of the range of vitamins and minerals found in wheat. At nearly every meal, there will be some form of bread served, be it a muffin or pancake for breakfast, sandwiches for lunch, or a roll at dinner.

I make all of the breads we eat in this house by hand. This cookbook is not the kind of comprehensive collection of several different kinds of breads so that you could pull it out and look up almost any kind of bread recipe. **What it is instead** is the collection of grain recipes that I use**, that I make for my family, on a regular basis**.

It ranges from Honey Oatmeal bread to Blueberry Muffins to Tortillas to Cornbread Stuffing and a host of recipes in between. All of the flours used are fresh ground (see more on that in the INGREDIENTS section of this book).

EQUIPMENT

I made the decision long ago not to hand-knead my bread dough. I did this for a couple of reasons. First, all the breads I ever made by kneading by hand turned out kind of heavy and dense – without exception. Second, what you must do for 10 minutes by hand can be done in 2 minutes by a stand mixer.

For a few years I used my stand mixer for kneading. I don't know that it was designed to be put through that kind of use on nearly a daily basis because I burned out the motor in it. After a hefty repair bill, I decided to use a bread machine that I had on hand (but had never used) to do everything but actually bake the bread. I don't like the shape of the final loaf the bread machines make, but my machine has a setting to just make the dough. After the first rise it will end the cycle. Bread machine motors were designed exclusively for kneading dough, and after a year of using it on a nearly daily basis, I'm not noticing that the motor is getting worn on any level.

So, while the recipes in this book all call for stand mixer mixing and kneading, and there are instructions on how to knead by hand, I typically put all of my bread ingredients into my bread machine and let it make the dough for me. I layer the ingredients – liquid, yeast, sweetener, etc., go on the bottom – followed by the flour and then any other ingredient such as salt, oats, etc.

YOU ARE WHAT YOU EAT: INGREDIENTS

While the title and introduction of this book are meant to be fun and a parody, the recipes are absolutely real. I find no greater way to show my love to my friends and family than to provide them with amazing food created with good ingredients. There are three main principles I follow in cooking:

1. Eat only substances God created for food. Avoid what is not designed for food.

2. As much as possible, eat foods as they were created – before they were changed or converted into something humans think might be better.

3. Avoid food addictions. Let no food or drink become your god.

In keeping with these three principles, nearly everything I cook I make from scratch. While this notion may sound odd to modern readers, cooking with fresh, whole, organically and locally grown food was common and "normal" until as recently as just 25 years ago.

I grind my own wheat to make flour. Every recipe in this book is made with fresh ground flour. I use either soft white wheat berries (for "quick" breads and pastries), or a combination of hard red and hard white wheat berries (for yeast breads). However, this is not the same as whole wheat flour found in the grocery stores. Store-bought whole wheat flour will not act the same, and store bought processed "enriched" white flour is incredibly bad for human health. So, experiment with flours and see what works and what doesn't work for you. Make adjustments. It may be that you have to mix whole wheat and white flours to make the recipes work for you.

When purchasing supplies, look for "aluminum free" baking powder. One of the reasons I use aluminum free is because I don't really want to be consuming the metal. But, another major reason to use it is because it will drastically improve the taste of your end product. Baking powder with aluminum creates a "tinny" taste that some palates pick up on right away.

When you're stocking ingredients for bread baking, one thing to be aware of is how unevenly priced yeast is. If you plan to make bread on a regular basis, it's SIGNIFICANTLY cheaper to buy a block of yeast ① from a baker's store or a shopping club (like Sam's or Costco) than it is to purchase individual packets of yeast. Each yeast packet contains 2 $\frac{1}{4}$ tsp of yeast – and each recipe will be marked accordingly.

Whenever milk is called for in a recipe, I use whole milk ①. I either use fresh raw milk or else non-homogenized organic milk. I do not cook with milk that has lower fat content than whole. If you do, you may need to adjust your recipe accordingly.

Whenever I refer to butter, I am talking about actual butter from an actual cow, never substitutes. Butter should be unsalted, real butter. I do not cook with salted butter or any kind of margarine or any kind of "buttery spread".

I do my best to avoid genetically modified foods (GMOs). Topping the list of GMOs are corn, soy, and canola. This is why, when a recipe calls for corn meal, I always recommend using organic meal, because in order to be labeled organic in the United States, it also cannot be GMO. I actually grind my own cornmeal from organic popcorn. If you have a grain mill, you can too.

I use extra virgin olive oil almost exclusively in my cooking. At time of print for this cookbook, organic canola oil is incredibly expensive. Generically labeled "vegetable oil" is almost always genetically modified (GMO) corn oil or processed and/or genetically modified soy oil or a combination of the two. Any kind of processed soy ⓘ, even from organic soy bean, is very toxic to men and boys and not really recommended for girls and women either!

On my Hallee the Homemaker website, I list the "Dirty Dozen ⓘ" – that is, the top GMO foods and the foods you should always try to purchase as certified organic if you don't grow your own or have access to a trusted sustainable local farm.

The "Dirty Dozen" foods that are the most contaminated on average are:

1 Peaches	5 Nectarines	9 Grapes (imported)
2 Apples	6 Strawberries	10 Pears
3 Sweet Bell Peppers	7 Cherries	11 Spinach
4 Celery	8 Lettuce	12 Potatoes

Probably the thing you'll notice most throughout this cookbook is that I never cook with pork. My family follows a Levitical Diet ⓘ – in that we don't eat foods that are specifically prohibited by the Bible. This means pork and bottom feeders like catfish and all shellfish are out.

The truth is we don't miss pork. Turkey breakfast sausage is a favorite in our home as is beef bacon. Turkey ham is a substitute that works in moderation for ham. And beef bacon is amazing and wonderfully versatile – as well as better tasting than any pork bacon any of us ever tasted.

ⓘ For more information on the world wide web, visit:

http://www.halleethehomemaker.com/2010/10/tip-saving-money-on-yeast/
http://www.halleethehomemaker.com/2011/04/the-dirty-dozen/
http://www.halleethehomemaker.com/levitical-diet/
http://www.halleethehomemaker.com/2009/09/soy-oh-boy/
http://www.halleethehomemaker.com/2012/10/milk-it-does-a-body-good/

YEAST BREADS

Few aromas are more comforting to me than that of fresh yeast bread baking in the oven. The smell surrounds me, comforts me, gives me a warm feeling inside of home and hearth.

Yeast bread baking can be intimidating. I know people who are convinced that they will never be able to "make" yeast do what it's supposed to do. However, for centuries, bread was prepared in the home on a regular basis. Every culture has some sort of bread that defines them. Our culture has lost the art of bread baking and instead we're raising an entire generation that believes bread comes in plastic bags from a shelf in the grocery store.

The yeast breads that follow in this book are breads that I make all the time. It is so exceedingly rare for me to go to a store and purchase bagged bread because I have sought out and perfected recipes for nearly every kind of bread we would want to consume on any kind of regular basis.

Before you venture forth into making these recipes, though, please note my discussion of ingredients in a previous section. One of the keys to a wonderful, successful loaf of bread is good, quality ingredients.

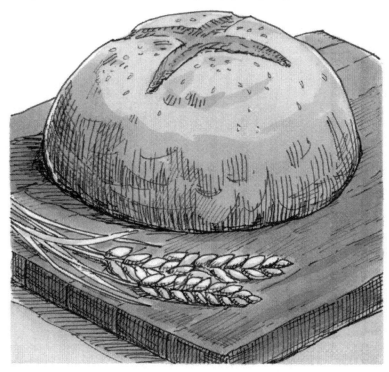

HONEY OATMEAL BREAD

Pleasant words are as an honeycomb, sweet to the soul, and health to the bones. Proverbs 16:24

Honey is often referred to as "nature's perfect food." Civilizations throughout history mastered bee keeping and used honey both as a food and as medicine. In Egypt, it was even used as a form of currency. Historically, it was used to make cement, preserve foods and even make furniture polish. It also doesn't appear to ever go bad. An archeologist found a jar of honey in an Egyptian tomb – the 3,300 year-old-jar of honey was still in good condition.

I love honey. I love cooking with honey in all extremes. I mean – how can you not love baklava? But in a less in-your-face nature's sweet goodness, I love this bread recipe.

This is the bread that is a major favorite of my family's. It's slightly sweet and light and the honey helps absorb and retain moisture, so it keeps these loaves fresh and moist.

My son, eat thou honey, because it is good; and the honeycomb, which is sweet to thy taste. Proverbs 24:13

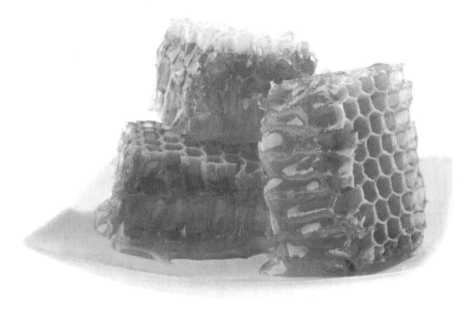

INGREDIENTS:

1 $\frac{1}{2}$ cups water

$\frac{1}{2}$ cup honey (pure, raw, local honey is always best)

$\frac{1}{8}$ cup butter

5 $\frac{1}{2}$ to 6 $\frac{1}{2}$ cups flour (I use a combination of fresh ground hard red and hard white wheat)

1 cup rolled oats

2 teaspoons Kosher or Sea salt

2 packages (4 $\frac{1}{2}$ teaspoons) active dry yeast

2 eggs

SUPPLIES:

two large bowls

measuring cups and spoons

wooden spoon or stand mixer with dough hook attachment

small saucepan

thermometer if desired

rolling pin

2 bread pans

towel to cover bowl while dough is rising

PREPARATION:

lightly grease a large bowl to use for rising the bread

DIRECTIONS:

Place water, honey, and butter in small saucepan. Heat over low heat until mixture is very warm (120° degrees F to 130° degrees F or 50° degrees C to 55° degrees C)

In a large mixing bowl, mix oats, 5 cups of flour, salt, and yeast.

When it's mixed, add the warm honey mixture. Then, mix until well mixed.

If you're using a stand mixer, mix it for about a minute. Add eggs and mix thoroughly. The dough will be very wet and sticky.

Add more flour, about half a cup at a time, until dough is manageable. If you're using a stand mixer, it should just start to clean the sides of the bowl. The dough should still be slightly sticky – not dry.

Put on lightly floured surface and knead for 10 minutes. Or, using a dough hook with your stand mixer, mix on speed 2 for 2 to 3 minutes.

Once the dough becomes smooth and elastic, put it into a lightly greased bowl. Turn it once and cover with a light towel. Let it sit in a warm spot until it doubles in bulk. It will take about an hour.

Punch the dough down and divide in half. Roll dough into a rectangle and roll up tightly.

Pinch the ends and place in a greased loaf pan. Cover and let rise in a warm place until nearly double in size.

Bake at 375° degrees F (190° degrees C) for 20-25 minutes. When you tap the loaf, if it sounds hollow, it's done. Remove from pans and immediately place on cooling racks.

 YIELD:

Two loaves

 NUTRITION:

Nutrition Facts	
Serving Size 94 g	
Amount Per Serving	
Calories 244	Calories from Fat 25
	% Daily Value*
Total Fat 2.8g	4%
Saturated Fat 1.2g	6%
Cholesterol 24mg	8%
Sodium 311mg	13%
Total Carbohydrates 48.2g	16%
Dietary Fiber 2.0g	8%
Sugars 8.2g	
Protein 6.6g	
Vitamin A 1% •	Vitamin C 0%
Calcium 1% •	Iron 15%
* Based on a 2000 calorie diet	

High in selenium

High in thiamin

 NOTES:

When adding the honey, if you have a source of local, pure, raw honey ask for the honey comb as well. Including the comb is good for you because consuming the comb increases your resistance to local allergens. And, in this case, I find that it makes for a more moist, melts-in-your mouth bread upon completion.

Often, yeast will not proof well in certain types of metal or plastic containers. Glass is best because it is nonporous, but ceramic or enamel also works.

How to knead dough by hand: Go to the link below to see a YouTube video with detailed instructions on how to knead dough by hand:
http://www.youtube.com/watch?v=dWj8oHMPFm0

WHOLE GRAIN WHEAT BREAD

This is the bread I make for my family's daily use. It's moist, light, and not too sweet. It cooks into toast well and slices easily for a sandwich. It keeps well in the bread box and travels well in lunch boxes. This is my "go to" bread.

 INGREDIENTS:

$^1/_3$ cup plus 1 TBS honey (pure, raw, local honey is always best)

2 cups warm water

4 $^1/_2$ tsp dry yeast (2 packets)

5 to 6 cups flour (I use a combination of fresh ground hard red and hard white wheat)

$^3/_4$ cup powdered milk

2 teaspoons salt (Kosher or Sea salt is best)

$^1/_3$ cup butter

 SUPPLIES:

two large bowls

measuring cups and spoons

wooden spoon or stand mixer with dough hook attachment

small saucepan

thermometer if desired

rolling pin

2 bread pans

towel to cover bowl while dough is rising

 PREPARATION:

Lightly grease a large bowl to use for rising the bread

Melt the butter

 DIRECTIONS:

Mix 1 TBS honey with warm water. Add yest. Let stand for 5 minutes.

Place 4 cups flour, the dry milk and salt in large bowl. Blend until well mixed. If using your stand mixture, turn on to speed 2 and add the remaining honey and the water/yeast mixture. Add the melted butter. (If mixing by

hand, mix well)

Add remaining flour $\frac{1}{2}$ cup at a time until the dough is no longer sticky.

Knead with the stand mixer for 2 minutes, or knead by hand for 10 minutes.

Once the dough becomes smooth and elastic, put it into a lightly greased bowl. Turn it once and cover with a light towel. Let it sit in a warm spot until it doubles in bulk. It will take about an hour.

Punch the dough down and divide in half. Roll dough into a rectangle and roll up tightly.

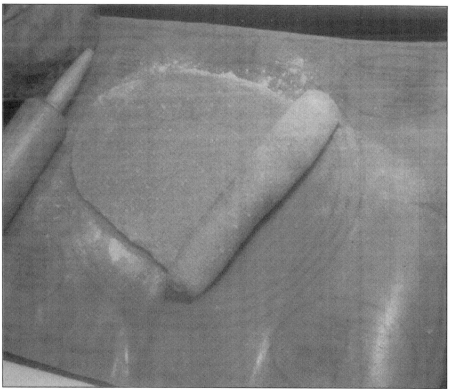

Pinch the ends and place in a greased loaf pan. Cover and let rise in a warm place until nearly double in size.

Bake at 400° degrees F (205° degrees C) for 15 minutes. Reduce the temperature to 350° degrees F (180° degrees C) and bake 20 to 30 minutes longer When you tap the loaf, if it sounds hollow, it's done. Remove from pans and immediately place on cooling racks.

YIELD:

two loaves

NUTRITION:

Nutrition Facts	
Serving Size 90 g	

Amount Per Serving	
Calories 226	Calories from Fat 38
	% Daily Value*
Total Fat 4.3g	7%
Saturated Fat 2.5g	13%
Trans Fat 0.0g	
Cholesterol 12mg	4%
Sodium 353mg	15%
Total Carbohydrates 40.2g	13%
Dietary Fiber 1.3g	5%
Sugars 9.4g	
Protein 6.8g	
Vitamin A 2% •	Vitamin C 1%
Calcium 8% •	Iron 11%
* Based on a 2000 calorie diet	

High in selenium

High in thiamin

NOTES:

Often, yeast will not proof well in certain types of metal or plastic containers. Glass is best because it is nonporous, but ceramic or enamel also works.

When adding the honey, if you have a source of local raw honey ask for the honey comb as well. Including the comb is good for you and, in this case, I find that it makes for a more moist bread upon completion.

How to knead dough by hand: Go to the link below to see a YouTube video with detailed instructions on how to knead dough by hand:
http://www.youtube.com/watch?v=dWj8oHMPFm0

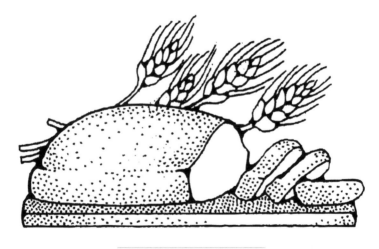

FABULOUS FRENCH BREAD

I use French Bread to serve with a meal, to make garlic bread, to make travel sandwiches, to make French toast … I love this bread. It is one of the easiest bread recipes I've ever come across. This recipe makes a light loaf that is just the right amount of crispy on the outside and soft on the inside.

INGREDIENTS:

4 $^1/_2$ tsp dry yeast (2 packages active dry yeast)
2 $^1/_2$ cups warm water (120° to 130° degrees F or 50° to 55° degrees C)
1 TBS Kosher or Sea salt
1 TBS extra virgin olive oil
7 cups flour (I use a combination of fresh ground hard red and hard white wheat)
2 TBS cornmeal
extra virgin olive oil

SUPPLIES:

two large bowls
wooden spoon OR stand mixer
measuring cups and spoons
rolling pin
baking sheet or French bread pan
towel to cover bowl while rising

PREPARATION:

Grease one large bowl with a light coating of extra virgin olive oil.

Temper (warm) your mixing bowl by filling it with hot tap water and dumping out.

DIRECTIONS:

Mix the water and the yeast in the warmed bowl. Let stand for 5 minutes. Add salt, oil, and flour. Mix well. (If using a stand mixer, mix for about a minute.)

On a floured surface, knead for 10 minutes. (If using a stand mixer, knead for 2 minutes on power level 2.)

Dough should be smooth and elastic.

Place in a greased bowl turn to grease top. Cover. Let rise in a warm place for about an hour.

Punch dough down and divide in half. Roll each half into 12 x 15 inch rectangle. Roll tightly from longest side. Tuck ends under.

Grease baking sheets and sprinkle with cornmeal. Place the rolled dough on baking sheet. (I have French bread pans that have little holes all through them, providing ventilation for the heat and making it unnecessary to sprinkle the pan with cornmeal.) Cut small slits diagonally in the top.

Cover and let rise for about an hour.

Bake 450° degrees F (230° degrees C) for 25-35 minutes. Bread is done when you tap it and it sounds hollow.

 YIELD:

Makes 2 loaves.

 NUTRITION:

Nutrition Facts	
Serving Size 96 g	
Amount Per Serving	
Calories 213	Calories from Fat 14
	% Daily Value*
Total Fat 1.5g	2%
Cholesterol 0mg	0%
Sodium 441mg	18%
Total Carbohydrates 42.9g	14%
Dietary Fiber 1.8g	7%
Protein 6.2g	
Vitamin A 0% •	Vitamin C 0%
Calcium 1% •	Iron 15%
* Based on a 2000 calorie diet	

Very low in cholesterol

Very low in sugar

Low in saturated fat

High in selenium

High in thiamin

 NOTES:

Often, yeast will not proof well in certain types of metal or plastic containers. Glass is best because it is nonporous, but ceramic or enamel also works.

How to knead dough by hand: Go to the link below to see a YouTube video with detailed instructions on how to knead dough by hand:

http://www.youtube.com/watch?v=dWj8oHMPFm0

SOAKED BREAD BOWLS

I created these bread bowls because my daughter wanted to eat broccoli cheese soup inside a bread bowl like she had at a restaurant one time. These were really good – when I originally made the recipe, I made six small bowls because I was feeding mostly children at the time. I think if you were feeding more adults than children you'd want to make four bowls per batch.

INGREDIENTS:

2 ¹/₂ cups warm water (120° to 130° degrees F or 50° to 55° degrees C)
7 cups flour (I used a combination of fresh ground hard red wheat and hard white wheat)
1 TBS buttermilk
1 TBS salt (Kosher or Sea salt is best)
1 TBS extra virgin olive oil
About 1 TBS cornmeal
1 egg white

SUPPLIES:

two large bowls

wooden spoon OR stand mixer

measuring cups and spoons

rolling pin

Baking

towel to cover bowl while rising

PREPARATION:

Mix the flour, water, and buttermilk together in a bowl. Cover and let stand overnight.

Grease one large bowl with a light coating of extra virgin olive oil

DIRECTIONS:

To the soaked dough, add the salt, yeast, and oil. Mix until thoroughly mixed. Knead for 10 minutes by hand or 2 minutes at speed 2 with a stand mixer.

Dough will be slightly sticky.

Place in a greased bowl turn to grease top. Cover. Let rise in a warm place for about an hour.

Punch dough down. Divide into half, and divide each half into thirds, for a total of six parts.

Sprinkle baking sheet or pizza stone with cornmeal.

Roll each piece into a ball and set on cornmeal on pan or stone. Cover with a light towel and let rise for about an hour.

Bake 450° degrees F (230° degrees C) for 15 minutes. Pull out of the oven and brush with beaten egg white, then return to the oven for another 10 to 15 minutes. They should be quite brown (browner than if they were just dinner rolls or loaves of bread.)

To serve, cut a circle out of the top and scoop out part of the bread inside, then fill with your favorite soup.

YIELD:

6 servings

NUTRITION:

Nutrition Facts

Serving Size 97 g

Amount Per Serving

Calories 210	Calories from Fat 13
	% Daily Value*
Total Fat 1.5g	2%
Cholesterol 0mg	0%
Sodium 445mg	19%
Total Carbohydrates 42.2g	14%
Dietary Fiber 1.5g	6%
Protein 5.9g	

Vitamin A 0%	•	Vitamin C 0%
Calcium 1%	•	Iron 14%

* Based on a 2000 calorie diet

Very low in cholesterol

Very low in sugar

Low in saturated fat

High in selenium

High in thiamin

NOTES:

Often, yeast will not proof well in certain types of metal or plastic containers. Glass is best because it is nonporous, but ceramic or enamel also works.

How to knead dough by hand: Go to the link below to see a YouTube video with detailed instructions on how to knead dough by hand:

http://www.youtube.com/watch?v=dWj8oHMPFm0

WHOLE WHEAT SOURDOUGH BREAD

This is a sourdough recipe that includes the starter. This is one of the simplest sourdough recipes I've ever come across. Sourdough is one of my favorite breads, and I was thrilled to discover a recipe that uses all fresh ground flour and not white flour.

I placed this in the "Yeast Breads" section even though there is no yeast included in the ingredients, because yeast occurs naturally and that is how sourdough rises even though you're not the one adding it. The key to sourdoughs like this one and Friendship breads is to cultivate your own, regional, naturally occurring yeasts with your "starter" and that is why sourdoughs in different regions have distinctive flavors.

San Francisco sourdough, Lancaster County Friendship bread, and New York City Bagels all have distinctive flavors because all of them have uniquely regional naturally occurring yeasts.

INGREDIENTS:

FOR THE STARTER:

$^3/_4$ cup flour (I use a combination of fresh ground hard red and hard white wheat)

$^3/_4$ cup warm water

FOR THE DOUGH:

6 cups flour (I use a combination of fresh ground hard red and hard white wheat)

2 cups hot water

2 tsp salt (Kosher or sea salt is best)

2 TBS extra virgin olive oil

 SUPPLIES:

Small glass or ceramic bowl for starter

Large bowl for mixing dough

Baking sheet

Measuring cups/spoons

 PREPARATION:

Mix flour with water into a small glass or ceramic bowl (I use a wide mouth pint-sized mason jar) and leave uncovered in a warm place.

After 24 hours, it's going to have a "skim" top.

Skim off the top, stir, and add about ¼ cup flour and ¼ cup warm water.

Repeat this for four days.

DIRECTIONS:

Mix the flour, water, and salt in the bowl. Add the starter mixture. Mix to form a dough. Knead until the dough is smooth – for at least 10 minutes by hand or 3 minutes with stand mixer and dough hook.

Pull out a golfball sized ball of dough to keep your starter going. Mix it with $^1/_4$ cup flour and $^1/_4$ cup warm water.

Place in a bowl and cover all over with the olive oil.

Let it sit for a minimum of four hours or as long as 24 hours or until it rises.

Preheat the oven to 350° degrees F (180° degrees C).

On a lightly floured surface, knead the dough and shape into two small loaves. Place on a baking sheet and bake for 1 hour.

YIELD:

2 small loaves

12 servings

NUTRITION:

Nutrition Facts

Serving Size 99 g

Amount Per Serving	
Calories 126	Calories from Fat 6
	% Daily Value*
Total Fat 0.7g	1%
Cholesterol 0mg	0%
Sodium 189mg	8%
Total Carbohydrates 25.8g	9%
Dietary Fiber 0.9g	4%
Protein 3.5g	
Vitamin A 0% •	Vitamin C 0%
Calcium 1% •	Iron 9%
* Based on a 2000 calorie diet	

Low in saturated fat

No cholesterol

Very low in sugar

High in selenium

High in thiamin

NOTES:

How to knead dough by hand: Go to the link below to see a YouTube video with detailed instructions on how to knead dough by hand:

http://www.youtube.com/watch?v=dWj8oHMPFm0

CRUSTY CHEESE BREAD

The herbs in this dough are very light – just enough to enhance the flavor of the cheese. A slice of this bread is the perfect side to almost any variety of soup of chili.

It is absolutely light and delicious. I recommend making a large batch because it won't go to waste.

INGREDIENTS:

4 ¹/₂ tsp yeast (2 packages active dry yeast)

1 cup warm water (should feel warm to the touch – if it feels hot, it's too hot)

5-5 ¹/₂ cups flour (I use a combination of fresh ground hard white and hard red wheat)

2 TBS honey (pure, raw, local honey is always best)

2 tsp salt (Kosher or sea salt is best)

2 TBS unsalted butter (softened)

1 cup warm whole milk (105° to 115° degrees F or 40° to 45° degrees C)

1 tsp garlic powder

2 tsp dried oregano

2 tsp dried parsley leaves

16 slices provolone cheese

SUPPLIES:

measuring cups/spoons

mixer or wooden spoon

2 large bowls

rolling pin

bread pans

PREPARATION:

Dissolve the yeast in the warm water.

Grease a large bowl and the bread pans.

DIRECTIONS:

Mix the flour, salt, honey, garlic, and herbs to bowl. Stir (or if using a stand mixer, mix on power level 2 with bread hook for 1 minute.) With the mixer running, gradually add the yeast and water mixture, warm milk, and softened butter. Mix on level 2 for about 2 minutes.

Add remaining flour, $\frac{1}{2}$ cup at a time until the dough is no longer sticking to the side of the bowl. Don't use all of the flour in the recipe unless you need it – the amount of flour used will be dependent upon the moisture content of your flour.

Knead dough for 2 minutes on power level 2 (or knead by hand for 10 minutes or until smooth and elastic.) Place in greased bowl, turning over to grease the top. Cover with a towel and let rise in a warm place, free from draft, for one hour or until doubled in bulk.

Punch dough down and divide in half. Place one ball of the dough on a floured surface and roll into a rectangle approximately 9x14 inches. Evenly distribute 8 slices of provolone cheese. Starting at the short end, roll the dough tightly. Pinch the ends. Place in greased bread pan.

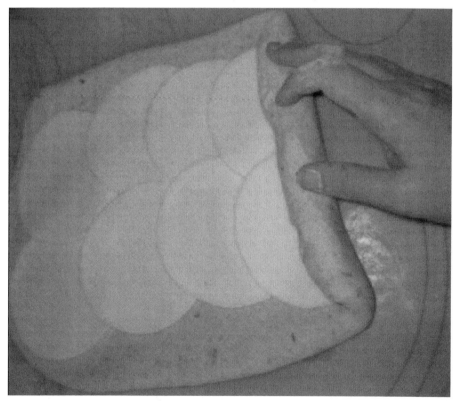

Repeat with the second ball of dough. Cover and let rise for one hour or until doubled.

When you have about 10 minutes of rising time left, preheat oven to 375° degrees F (190° degrees C).

Bake each loaf for about 40 minutes, or until browned. Remove from pans and cool on a wire cooling rack.

 YIELD:

2 loaves

 NUTRITION:

Nutrition Facts	
Serving Size 108 g	
Amount Per Serving	
Calories 289	Calories from Fat 89
	% Daily Value*
Total Fat 9.9g	15%
Saturated Fat 6.1g	30%
Cholesterol 25mg	8%
Sodium 554mg	23%
Total Carbohydrates 36.9g	12%
Dietary Fiber 1.5g	6%
Sugars 3.1g	
Protein 12.6g	
Vitamin A 7% •	Vitamin C 1%
Calcium 24% •	Iron 13%
* Based on a 2000 calorie diet	

High in selenium

 NOTES:

If you don't have Provolone cheese, you can experiment with other cheeses. Personally, I found fresh Mozzerella to work, but not as well as Provolone. Cheddar and Colby didn't aesthetically do very well, but they tasted quite good.

Remember that often, yeast will not proof well in certain types of metal or plastic containers. Glass is best because it is nonporous, but ceramic or enamel also works.

How to knead dough by hand: Go to the link below to see a YouTube video with detailed instructions on how to knead dough by hand:
http://www.youtube.com/watch?v=dWj8oHMPFm0

SCRUMPTIOUS CINNAMON SWIRL BREAD

I LOVE cinnamon mixed with almost anything bready. I confess it is a weakness of mine. This bread is wonderful – and I am so very pleased that it relies upon honey to sweeten instead of sugar. This bread makes amazing Family Favorite French Toast, or if you can't wait for a breakfast morning, you can just dive right into it and eat it fresh and warm from the oven, plain or maybe with a pat of softened butter.

Two loaves never last long in my house. This bread also makes a wonderful gift. The fresh, homey fragrance of baked yeast and cinnamon will make anyone feel loved and appreciated.

INGREDIENTS:

FOR THE DOUGH:
4 $^1/_2$ tsp yeast (2 packages active dry yeast)

1 cup warm water (should feel warm to the touch – if it feels hot, it's too hot)

5-5 $^1/_2$ cups flour (I combine fresh ground hard white and hard red wheat)

2 TBS honey (pure, raw, local honey is always best)

2 tsp salt (Kosher or sea salt is best)

2 TBS unsalted butter (softened)

1 cup warm whole milk (105° to 115° degrees F or 40° to 45° degrees C)

FOR THE FILLING:
$^2/_3$ cup honey ($^1/_3$ cup for each loaf)

At least 2 TBS cinnamon (generous amount – quantity to taste)

1 cup raisins (optional)

SUPPLIES:

measuring cups/spoons

mixer or wooden spoon

2 large bowls

rolling pin

bread pans

PREPARATION:

Dissolve the yeast in the warm water.

Grease a large bowl and the bread pans.

DIRECTIONS:

Mix the flour, honey, and salt. Stir (or if using a stand mixer, mix on power level 2 with bread hook for 1 minute.) With the mixer running, gradually add the yeast and water mixture, warm milk, and softened butter. Mix on level 2 for about 2 minutes.

Add remaining flour, $^1/_2$ cup at a time until the dough is no longer sticking to the side of the bowl. Don't use all of the flour in the recipe unless you need it – the amount of flour used will be dependent upon the moisture content of your flour.

Knead dough for 2 minutes on power level 2 (or knead by hand for 10 minutes or until smooth and elastic.) Place in greased bowl, turning over to grease the top. Cover with a towel and let rise in a warm place, free from draft, for one hour or until doubled in bulk.

Punch dough down and divide in half. Place one ball of the dough on a floured surface and roll into a rectangle approximately 9x14 inches. Evenly spread $\frac{1}{3}$ cup honey, not quite to the edges. Sprinkle generously with cinnamon and $\frac{1}{2}$ cup raisins, if desired. Starting at the short end, roll the dough tightly. Pinch the ends. Place in greased bread pan.

Repeat with the second ball of dough. Cover and let rise for one hour or until doubled.

When you have about 10 minutes of rising time left, preheat oven to 375° degrees F (190° degrees C).

Bake each loaf for about 40 minutes, or until browned. Remove from pans and cool on a wire cooling rack.

 YIELD:

2 loaves

 NUTRITION:

Nutrition Facts	
Serving Size 103 g	
Amount Per Serving	
Calories 262	Calories from Fat 22
	% Daily Value*
Total Fat 2.5g	4%
Saturated Fat 1.3g	6%
Trans Fat 0.0g	
Cholesterol 5mg	2%
Sodium 311mg	13%
Total Carbohydrates 55.6g	19%
Dietary Fiber 2.2g	9%
Sugars 20.1g	
Protein 5.7g	
Vitamin A 1% •	Vitamin C 1%
Calcium 4% •	Iron 14%
* Based on a 2000 calorie diet	

Very low in cholesterol

High in antioxidants

 NOTES:

For a nutty, artisan flavor, you can also add $\frac{1}{2}$ cup (each loaf) of chopped walnuts or pecans along with the raisins.

Often, yeast will not proof well in certain types of metal or plastic containers. Glass is best because it is nonporous, but ceramic or enamel also works.

How to knead dough by hand: Go to the link below to see a YouTube video with detailed instructions on how to knead dough by hand:

http://www.youtube.com/watch?v=dWj8oHMPFm0

GRANNY EVERMAN'S YEAST ROLLS

These rolls are a favorite whenever they are served. We make them in large batches for every evening meal at the youth camp we support every year. They are slightly sweet, light and delicious.

INGREDIENTS:

4 $^1/_2$ tsp (2 pkgs.) dry yeast

2 $^1/_2$ cups water, divided

2 tsp salt

1 tsp honey and also $^3/_4$ cup honey (pure, raw, local honey is always best)

5 cups flour (I use a combination of fresh ground hard white and hard red wheat)

$^1/_2$ cup safflower oil (or organic canola)

SUPPLIES:

Measuring cups/spoons

Glass, ceramic, or enamel bowl to proof yeast

Rolling pin and floured workspace

Biscuit cutter (clean, dry large soup can or medium drinking cup also works)

cookie sheet or baking pan

PREPARATION:

Make sure you have time to bake. Each rise takes about 2 hours for a total of 4 hours. Also, you will need to preheat the oven to 400° degrees F prior to baking and each batch will need to bake for about 20 minutes.

DIRECTIONS:

Mix 2 packages of dry yeast in 2 cups of warm water in an enamel, ceramic, or glass* bowl. Stir until yeast is dissolved. Set aside.

Mix salt and 1 tsp honey in $^1/_2$ cup lukewarm water and stir until dissolved. Set aside.

Put the flour in a large bowl To the yeast mixture, add the honey/salt mixture. Stir in oil and honey. Combine with the flour until you get a soft dough. (You may need to add a little more flour.)

Let rise for 2 hours for your first rise and punch it down.

NOTE: When you make a big batch of this recipe, you can save a portion of it in the freezer. After it rises the first time and you punch down the dough, break off however much you want to save. Put it in a freezer bag, make sure you remove all of the air, and label it "yeast roll dough" so you know what it is. The night before you're going to make rolls again, remove the dough from the freezer and put it in the refrigerator to thaw. Remove it from the refrigerator and bring it to room temperature before using. The end result is identical.

On lightly floured surface, roll until about $^3/_4$ inch thick and cut with a round biscuit cutter (or a wide-mouth glass or jar). Place on greased pan. Let rise for 2 hours.

Bake in preheated 400° degrees F (205° degrees C) oven for 20 minutes or until golden

 YIELD:

Makes about 24 good sized yeast rolls.

 NUTRITION:

Nutrition Facts	
Serving Size 101 g	
Amount Per Serving	
Calories 255	Calories from Fat 65
	% Daily Value*
Total Fat 7.2g	11%
Cholesterol 0mg	0%
Sodium 294mg	12%
Potassium 73mg	2%
Total Carbohydrates 43.7g	15%
Dietary Fiber 1.3g	5%
Sugars 13.5g	
Protein 4.5g	
Vitamin A 0%	Vitamin C 0%
Calcium 1%	Iron 12%
Nutrition Grade B	
* Based on a 2000 calorie diet	

Low in saturated fat

No cholesterol

 NOTES:

Often, yeast will not proof well in certain types of metal or plastic containers. Glass is best because it is nonporous, but ceramic or enamel also works. The better proof you get on the yeast, the lighter and fluffier these rolls will turn out.

PULL APART YEAST ROLLS

These rolls were light and wonderful – a perfect compliment to your holiday feast – or any feast for that matter!

INGREDIENTS:

2 $\frac{1}{4}$ tsp yeast (1 package active dry yeast)

1 cup warm water (105° to 115° degrees F or 40° to 45° degrees C)

$\frac{1}{2}$ cup unsalted butter, divided

3-3 $\frac{1}{2}$ cups flour (I use a mixture of fresh ground hard red and hard white wheat)

2 TBS honey (pure, raw, local honey is always best)

1 $\frac{1}{2}$ tsp salt (Kosher or sea salt is best)

oil to grease the bowl for rising and the muffin tins.

SUPPLIES:

bowl

stand mixer with dough hook (if you're not going to knead by hand)

measuring cups/spoons

muffin tin

method by which you will melt butter (either glass bowl and microwave or a saucepan)

pizza cutter or sharp knife

PREPARATION:

Fill mixing bowl with hot water and dump out the water to warm the bowl.

Melt $\frac{1}{4}$ cup of the butter now, and know you'll need to melt the remaining $\frac{1}{4}$ cup of the butter after the first rise.

DIRECTIONS:

Dissolve the yeast in warmed mixing bowl in the water for 5 minutes.

Add $\frac{1}{4}$ cup of the melted butter, flour, honey, and salt.

Mix 1 minute with the dough hook in your your stand mixer on speed 2 (or stir) until well blended.

Continuing on speed 2, continue to add flour, $\frac{1}{2}$ cup at a time, until the dough starts to clean the sides of the bowl.

Mix (or knead) for 2 more minutes (or 10 minutes by hand on a floured surface) or until smooth and elastic.

Place in greased bowl.

Turn to coat it all in oil.

Cover and let rise for 1 hour or until doubled in bulk.

Put on lightly floured surface. Roll out into a 12x9 inch rectangle.

Brush with the remaining $\frac{1}{4}$ cup of butter. Cut into 6 strips, long ways (so that they are 12-inches long).

Stack the strips on top of each other. While stacked, cut into 12 pieces.

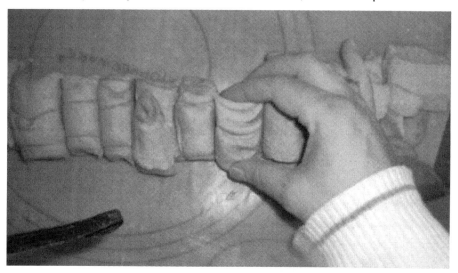

Place into greased muffin tins, cut side up. Cover and let rise about 45 minutes.

When they have about 10 minutes left to rise, preheat oven to 400° degrees F (205° degrees C).

Bake for 15 to 20 minutes or until nicely browned.

Remove immediately from pans.

YIELD:

12 rolls

NUTRITION:

Nutrition Facts	
Serving Size 94 g	
Amount Per Serving	
Calories 284	Calories from Fat 97
	% Daily Value*
Total Fat 10.8g	17%
Saturated Fat 6.6g	33%
Cholesterol 27mg	9%
Sodium 462mg	19%
Total Carbohydrates 41.3g	14%
Dietary Fiber 1.5g	6%
Sugars 3.7g	
Protein 5.5g	
Vitamin A 6% •	Vitamin C 0%
Calcium 1% •	Iron 14%
* Based on a 2000 calorie diet	

Low in sodium

No Trans Fats

NOTES:

If these directions don't make sense to you (like they didn't to me the first time I read them), just start working it and they will make sense. It's a lot easier on my blog when I have pictures to show the step-by-step. You can see the pictures for this recipe at this link:

Often, yeast will not proof well in certain types of metal or plastic containers. Glass is best because it is nonporous, but ceramic or enamel also works.

How to knead dough by hand: Go to the link below to see a YouTube video with detailed instructions on how to knead dough by hand:
http://www.youtube.com/watch?v=dWj8oHMPFm0

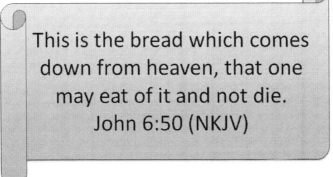

This is the bread which comes down from heaven, that one may eat of it and not die.
John 6:50 (NKJV)

LAURA'S WHOLE WHEAT HAMBURGER BUNS

I got this recipe from Laura Coppinger at Heavenly Homemakers ⓘ. Check out her wonderful website when you can. This recipe is super easy and the buns are so delicious.

INGREDIENTS:

5 (+) cups flour (I use a combination of fresh ground hard white and hard red wheat)

1 ½ cups warm water

2 pkgs regular or active dry yeast (4 ½ tsp)

2 TBS honey (pure, raw, local honey is always best)

¼ cup water

½ cup whole milk

2 TBS unsalted butter

2 tsp salt (Kosher or sea salt is best)

SUPPLIES:

bowl

wooden spoon

rolling pin

wide mouth jar or glass or large biscuit cutter to cut out the buns

cookie sheet on which to bake them

PREPARATION:

In a large mixing bowl, stir together 3 cups of whole wheat flour and 1½ cups warm water. Set aside to let rest for 30 minutes. In the meantime, mix together ¼ cup water, yeast and honey. Allow this to sit for at least 10 minutes to activate the yeast.

DIRECTIONS:

Melt butter, milk and salt in a small saucepan on the stove. Do not allow the mixture to get above 120°F.

Pour yeast mixture and milk mixture into flour mixture. Add remaining two cups of flour (more if needed).

Knead for about 10 minutes until dough begins to look "shiny". Put dough back into the bowl, cover and let rise for at least an hour...or until it has doubled.

Pull dough onto a clean countertop and knead for a couple of minutes to get any air bubbles out. Roll dough on a lightly floured surface until about 1/2 inch thick.

Cut circles from the dough with a large drinking glass or wide mouth jar. Place circles on in a well buttered baking dish about an inch apart.

Allow to rise for about 30 minutes. Bake for 20-25 minutes in a 350°F (180° C). degree oven.

YIELD:

Makes about 18 buns.

NUTRITION:

Nutrition Facts

Serving Size 90 g

Amount Per Serving	
Calories 195	Calories from Fat 22
	% Daily Value*
Total Fat 2.4g	4%
Saturated Fat 1.3g	6%
Cholesterol 5mg	2%
Sodium 351mg	15%
Total Carbohydrates 37.4g	12%
Dietary Fiber 1.5g	6%
Sugars 2.9g	
Protein 5.4g	
Vitamin A 1% •	Vitamin C 0%
Calcium 2% •	Iron 13%
* Based on a 2000 calorie diet	

Low in cholesterol

High in selenium

High in thiamin

NOTES:

You can shape them into hot dog buns shapes before they rise the second time and create hot dog buns as well.

To see Laura Coppinger's version of this recipe, visit her fabulous website at Heavenly Homemakers.

ⓘ http://heavenlyhomemakers.com/whole-wheat-hamburger-buns

PERFECT POCKET PITA BREAD

This recipe makes a nice pocket bread that you can stuff with yummy ingredients to make gyros, shwarmas, or fun PBJs for school functions.

INGREDIENTS:

3 cups flour (I use a combination of fresh ground hard white and hard red wheat)

1 $\frac{1}{2}$ tsp salt (Kosher or sea salt is best)

1 TBS honey (pure, raw, local honey is always best)

2 $\frac{1}{4}$ tsp dry yeast (1 packet active dry yeast)

1 $\frac{1}{4}$ to 1 $\frac{1}{2}$ cups room temperature water

2 TBS extra virgin olive oil

SUPPLIES:

bowl

measuring cup/spoons

wooden spoon

rolling pin

baking stone or cookie sheet

PREPARATION:

Mix yeast with honey and 1 $\frac{1}{4}$ cup water. Let stand 5 minutes.

DIRECTIONS:

Sift together flour and salt. Add to yeast mixture, add extra virgin olive oil. Stir with a wooden spoon until it forms a ball (adding more water if needed.) Place on lightly floured surface and knead for 10 minutes. (If you are using a stand mixer, using a bread hook mix for 3 minutes on speed 2.)

Place dough in greased glass bowl and turn it so that both sides are greased. Cover with a towel and let it rise in a warm spot free from drafts until doubled in size (60 to 90 minutes).

Punch dough down and divide into 8 pieces. Roll each piece into a ball. Cover with a towel and let rest for 20 minutes.

While the dough is resting, preheat oven to 400° degrees F (205° degrees C). Put either a baking stone (or an upside down cookie sheet) on the middle rack of the oven while it's preheating.

On a lightly floured surface, roll each ball of dough out to a $1/4$ inch thick.

Open the oven and place as many pitas as will fit on your baking surface (I typically do 2 at a time). Bake 3 minutes (when they puff up).

I will let the stone or baking sheet reheat for a couple of minutes before placing the next batch in the oven – that tends to give better results.

Serve with your favorite filling.

 YIELD:

8 pitas

 NUTRITION:

Nutrition Facts

Serving Size 100 g

Amount Per Serving	
Calories 211	Calories from Fat 36
	% Daily Value*
Total Fat 4.0g	6%
Saturated Fat 0.6g	3%
Cholesterol 0mg	0%
Sodium 441mg	18%
Total Carbohydrates 38.3g	13%
Dietary Fiber 1.5g	6%
Sugars 2.1g	
Protein 5.3g	
Vitamin A 0% •	Vitamin C 0%
Calcium 1% •	Iron 13%
* Based on a 2000 calorie diet	

Low in cholesterol

High in selenium

High in thiamin

 NOTES:

Using a cast iron skillet on top of a cast iron skillet, you can re-heat these and press them flat, then cut into fourths and serve with a Greek salad.

Often, yeast will not proof well in certain types of metal or plastic containers. Glass is best because it is nonporous, but ceramic or enamel also works.

How to knead dough by hand: Go to the link below to see a YouTube video with detailed instructions on how to knead dough by hand:

http://www.youtube.com/watch?v=dWj8oHMPFm0

GRAPE PEEL PITA BREAD

In ancient times, people had not yet discovered the properties of yeast, but knew that the fruit peel, and especially the peel of apples and grapes, fermented the bread dough and made it rise.

I originally tried this recipe during a period of fasting just to see how it worked, and was so pleasantly surprised by how good this bread tastes. In making this recipe in the last few years, I've grated grapes, which means that little tiny flecks of peel were in the bread. But, I've also used a juicer to juice the grapes, and it simply made a dark dough. Either way, this bread tastes slightly sweet and really delicious.

I placed this in the "Yeast Breads" section even though there is no yeast included in the ingredients, because yeast naturally occur on grape skins. That is how this bread rises even though you're not the one adding yeast.

INGREDIENTS:

$^1/_2$ to $^3/_4$ cups fresh grape juice

5 cups flour (I use a combination of fresh ground hard red and hard white wheat)

$^1/_4$ tsp salt (Kosher or Sea salt is best)

1 tsp extra virgin olive oil

SUPPLIES:

Grater, cup

Large bowl

Baking sheet or pizza stone

rolling pin

PREPARATION:

Prepare your grape skins according to your preference and available kitchen tools for the job.

Make grape juice by grating seedless grapes into a cup peel and all with a zester or grater, or place your grapes in a small food processor or blender and puree them down to juice peel and all, or put your grapes through a juicer and retain the peel.

DIRECTIONS:

Mix the flour, salt, and oil. Slowly add the grape juice, mixing well, until a dough is formed. Knead until the dough is smooth.

Let sit for 2 hours.

Knead for 5 minutes. Divide dough into 6 to 8 equally sized balls. Let rest.

While the dough is resting, preheat oven to 400° degrees F (205° degrees C). Put either a baking stone (or an upside down cookie sheet) on the middle rack of the oven while it's preheating.

On a lightly floured surface, roll each ball of dough out to a $\frac{1}{4}$ inch thick.

Open the oven and place as many pitas as will fit on your baking surface (I typically do 2 at a time). Bake 3 minutes.

I will let the stone or baking sheet reheat for a couple of minutes before placing the next batch in the oven — that tends to give better results.

Serve with your favorite filling.

YIELD:

6 to 8 servings

NUTRITION:

Nutrition Facts

Serving Size 102 g

Amount Per Serving	
Calories 298	Calories from Fat 12

	% Daily Value*
Total Fat 1.4g	2%
Cholesterol 0mg	0%
Sodium 75mg	3%
Total Carbohydrates 61.7g	21%
Dietary Fiber 2.1g	9%
Sugars 2.3g	
Protein 8.2g	

Vitamin A 0%	•	Vitamin C 11%
Calcium 1%	•	Iron 20%

* Based on a 2000 calorie diet

Very low in saturated fat

No cholesterol

Low in sodium

Low in sugar

High in selenium

High in thiamin

NOTES:

This bread keeps for a few days and is great for pita sandwiches, especially pita PBJs with grape jelly.

HOMEMADE PIZZA CRUST

My family loves homemade pizza. We top this with crust with all sorts of toppings – from a traditional tomato based pizza sauce to BBQ sauce to a white sauce. Once you have a good dough, you are kind of limitless with the toppings.

INGREDIENTS:

2 $\frac{1}{4}$ tsp dry yeast (1 pkg)
1 cup warm water (105° to 115° degrees F or 40° to 45° degrees C)
2 $\frac{1}{2}$ to 3 $\frac{1}{2}$ cups flour (I use a mixture of fresh ground hard red and hard white wheat)
$\frac{1}{2}$ tsp salt (Kosher or sea salt is best)
2 tsp extra virgin olive oil

SUPPLIES:

stand mixer (if you have one – or you can mix the dough by hand)
Measuring cups/spoons
pizza pans

PREPARATION:

Temper (warm) your mixing bowl by filling it with hot tap water and emptying it.

Lightly grease another bowl with olive oil.

DIRECTIONS:

Dissolve yeast in 1 cup of warm water in warmed mixing bowl for 5 minutes.

Add 2 cups of flour, the olive oil and salt. Mix (or stir) until blended.

Add remaining flour half a cup at a time until the dough is formed but still a little bit sticky. Knead for about 5 minutes, adding just a touch of flour to keep it from being too sticky to handle. If you're using a stand mixer, mix for about 2 minutes on speed 2.

Put dough in the greased bowl. Turn it so that the top is lightly greased as well.

Cover and let rise for 1 hour.

Using a paper towel dipped in olive oil, oil your pizza pans.

Divide the dough in two.

Pick up the dough and let it stretch out. Turn a half-turn and let it stretch. Turn a half turn and let it stretch some more. Keep working it until you get to about the size and shape of your pan. Put it in the pan and then carefully stretch and pat the dough until it covers the pan.

Top with your preferred sauce and toppings.

Bake at 450° degrees F (230° degrees C) for 15 to 20 minutes on the lowest rack in the oven.

 YIELD:

2 pizzas

 NUTRITION:

Nutrition Facts

Serving Size 87 g

Amount Per Serving

Calories 212	Calories from Fat 16

	% Daily Value*
Total Fat 1.8g	3%
Cholesterol 0mg	0%
Sodium 150mg	6%
Total Carbohydrates 42.2g	14%
Dietary Fiber 1.7g	7%
Protein 6.1g	

Vitamin A 0%	•	Vitamin C 0%
Calcium 1%	•	Iron 15%

* Based on a 2000 calorie diet

Very low in saturated fat

No cholesterol

Very low in sugar

High in selenium

High in thiamin

*Based on cheese pizza; additional toppings will change nutritional value.

 NOTES:

You can use any sauce, any topping, any cheese you want. Make your family's favorite and enjoy.

Often, yeast will not proof well in certain types of metal or plastic containers. Glass is best because it is nonporous, but ceramic or enamel also works.

How to knead dough by hand: Go to the link below to see a YouTube video with detailed instructions on how to knead dough by hand:
http://www.youtube.com/watch?v=dWj8oHMPFm0

GREEK LENTEN BREAD (LAGANA)

And he took bread, and gave thanks, and broke it, and gave unto them, saying, This is my body which is given for you: this do in remembrance of me. Luke 22:19

In Greek, *Kathari Deftera*, means Clean Monday (you may know it as Ash Monday), and it is the first day of the Orthodox Lent. The Lenten bread known as *Lagana* traditionally sees the light of day only once each year, on Clean Monday. Orthodox Lent is a moveable feast which always occurs forty-eight days prior to Resurrection Sunday (called Easter). It is a day of purification, both spiritual and physical, as the great fasting period begins.

Lagana was originally an unleavened bread but, over the years, a little yeast has crept into the recipes. It's most often shaped like a rectangle with rounded corners, and is a fairly flat loaf.

Orthodox Lenten restrictions dictate the use of extra virgin olive oil, although a substitute oil can be employed if you are not strictly observing. Personally, I feel the extra virgin olive oil lends Lagana its unique and internationally recognizable flavor, and it's healthier than most alternatives. This recipe is Daniel fast friendly, Orthodox fast friendly, and Lent friendly.

INGREDIENTS:

FOR THE BREAD:

4 cups flour (I use a mixture of fresh ground hard red and hard white wheat)

$^1/_2$ cup extra virgin olive oil

2 $^1/_4$ tsp dry yeast (1 packet active dry yeast)

$^1/_2$ tsp salt (Kosher or sea salt is best)

1 cup lukewarm water

FOR THE TOPPING:

extra virgin olive oil

4-5 TBS white sesame seeds

a few black sesame seeds

SUPPLIES:

measuring cups/spoons

mixing bowls

baking sheets: either cookie sheet or pizza stone

brush for extra virgin olive oil

PREPARATION:

When there is about 10 minutes left in the second rise, preheat the oven to 355° degrees F (180° degrees C)

DIRECTIONS:

Sprinkle the yeast in 1 cup of warm water in a nonreactive bowl. Leave sit for 30 minutes until it foams.

In a large bowl, whisk together the flour and salt. Make a well in the center and add the yeast-water mix and oil. With hands or a wooden spoon, mix to create a cohesive dough. If needed, add a little more warm water.

On a floured surface, knead the dough until it no longer sticks to the hands and is soft and malleable, about 10 minutes (or, using a dough hook, knead for 2 minutes on speed 2 with a stand mixture). Form into three flat loaves, round or rectangular, about $^1/_2$ to $^3/_4$ inch high.

Place on baking sheets, cover with a towel, and allow to sit until doubled in height, about 45 minutes.

Poke the loaves in several places with your fingers. Brush lightly with oil and sprinkle evenly with sesame seeds (approximately 1 tablespoon per loaf).

Bake at 355° degrees F (180° degrees C) for 30 to 40 minutes, until golden.

YIELD:

3 loaves

NUTRITION:

Nutrition Facts	
Serving Size 89 g	
Amount Per Serving	
Calories 288	Calories from Fat 108
	% Daily Value*
Total Fat 12.0g	19%
Saturated Fat 1.5g	8%
Trans Fat 0.0g	
Cholesterol 0mg	0%
Sodium 118mg	5%
Total Carbohydrates 39.0g	13%
Dietary Fiber 1.5g	6%
Protein 6.0g	
Vitamin A 0% •	Vitamin C 0%
Calcium 4% •	Iron 15%
* Based on a 2000 calorie diet	

Low in sodium

Very low in sugar

No cholesterol

NOTES:

In Greek: pronounce lah-GHAH-nah

Lagana loaves harden quickly so serve them the same day they are baked if you can. If you aren't planning to eat it immediately, cool the loaves completely, wrap in airtight plastic or seal-a-meal, and freeze. They will keep well in the freezer for several months.

Often, yeast will not proof well in certain types of metal or plastic containers. Glass is best because it is nonporous, but ceramic or enamel also works.

How to knead dough by hand: Go to the link below to see a YouTube video with detailed instructions on how to knead dough by hand:
http://www.youtube.com/watch?v=dWj8oHMPFm0

QUICK BREADS

I use the term "quick" only to define the rate at which these breads rise. Some recipes, like the Cinnamon Honey Scones with Raisins, have to soak overnight. However, in terms of this cookbook, "quick" simply means that you don't have to add yeast and wait for the dough to rise multiple times over the course of several hours.

Quick breads can be anything from pancakes for breakfast in the morning to my Grandma's Favorite Zucchini Bread and everything in between.

I scour "quick bread" recipes for breakfast foods and for different after school snacks.

Any of the recipes that follow which call for baking powder for use as a leavening specify *aluminum-free* baking powder. It is important to purchase and use only aluminum-free for two reasons. First, it tastes much, much better. Second, the long term health effects of consuming large amounts of industrial grade metals are still being debated. In some studies, aluminum intake has been linked to serious health problems.

SUE GREGG'S OATMEAL BLENDER WAFFLES/PANCAKES

Sue Gregg ⓘ is the master at "blender baking" and a wonderful resource for cooking with real food, whole food, Biblical food, gluten free food, and whole grains. I love her recipes so much that I bought every last one of her cookbooks. I cannot recommend them enough and they have pride of place in my cookbook collection.

Of all her wonderful recipes, this one is a definite favorite in our house.

This is a wonderful pancake/waffle recipe. I thought the oats would have less of a flavor – as in oatmeal bread – but they didn't. This tasted nutty and rich like … oatmeal! Cooked on the griddle they are filling and mouthwatering. Cooked in the waffle iron they are crisp on the outside and moist and rich on the inside. Of all the waffles I have ever had in my life, none top these. Dripping with butter and topped with real maple syrup they are simply wonderful!

It is an absolute pleasure to make this wonderful recipe for my family for breakfast from time to time. I have also found that a stack of these waffles is also a popular self serve breakfast when my daughter hosts a sleepover party. I serve them along with a side bar of fresh whipped cream, fresh organic berries, real maple syrup, chocolate syrup, powdered sugar, chocolate chips, and lots of softened butter. With breakfast meats, farm fresh eggs, hot coffee, cold milk and juice, to say these are a hit is an understatement.

They are also a perfect choice for a southern style Waffle & Fried Chicken dinner.

INGREDIENTS:

1 ¹/₂ – 1 ³/₄ cups liquid such as buttermilk or kefir (or non-dairy alternative)

some additional liquid (optional if batter needs thinning)

2 TBS extra virgin olive oil

1 tsp vanilla extract

1 ¹/₂ cups uncooked rolled oats

1 egg

2 tsp baking powder

¹/₂ tsp aluminum-free baking soda

1 tsp salt (Kosher or sea salt is best)

SUPPLIES:

measuring cups/spoons

blender

rubber spatula

waffle iron and tongs for waffles

–OR–

griddle and spatula for pancakes

PREPARATION:

THE NIGHT BEFORE:

Place buttermilk, olive oil, vanilla, and oats in blender.

The batter should always swirl into a vortex in the blender. If it doesn't, slowly add more liquid until the hole reappears.

NOTE: This is the secret to light and tender waffles. Batter for pancakes may be thicker, but keep batter relatively thin and keep it churning.

Cover blender and let stand at room temperature overnight or up to 12 to 24 hours.

DIRECTIONS:

Preheat waffle iron at highest temperature, or griddle on medium high.

Add egg to the blender and blend on high for 1 minute. If you need to add a little bit of buttermilk to keep the vortex going in the blender, that's fine.

Blend in the baking powder, baking soda, and salt just until blended.

Pour batter onto hot waffle iron, sprayed with extra virgin olive oil. Bake about 3 $\frac{1}{2}$ to 4 minutes in waffle iron until crispy.

– OR –

Pour onto hot griddle. Cook until bubbles pop on the surface, then flip and cook for about 1 to 2 minutes longer, or until browned.

YIELD:

About 5 to 7 good sized waffles, depending on waffle iron size, or about 10 to 12 good sized pancakes depending on pancake size.

NUTRITION:

Nutrition Facts	
Serving Size 108 g	
Amount Per Serving	
Calories 160	Calories from Fat 66
	% Daily Value*
Total Fat 7.4g	11%
Saturated Fat 1.5g	8%
Cholesterol 30mg	10%
Sodium 580mg	24%
Total Carbohydrates 18.2g	6%
Dietary Fiber 2.1g	8%
Sugars 3.8g	
Protein 6.0g	
Vitamin A 1% •	Vitamin C 1%
Calcium 17% •	Iron 7%
* Based on a 2000 calorie diet	

High in phosphorus

High in manganese

High in calcium

NOTES:

ⓘSue Gregg has an online demonstration of how to make this wonderful, healthy blender batter at this link:

http://www.suegregg.com/recipes/breakfasts/blenderbatterwaffles/blenderbatterwaffl erecipe.htm

ⓘSue Gregg's full recipe is here:

http://www.suegregg.com/recipes/breakfasts/blenderbatterwaffles/blenderbatterwaffl esA.htm

Consider adding Sue Gregg's wonderful cookbooks to your collection. Visit her website at www.suegregg.com to order.

FAMILY FAVORITE BUTTERMILK PANCAKES

Pancakes. Flapjacks. Griddlecakes. A hot steaming stack with butter melting down the sides is certainly an iconic image of the perfect breakfast food.

I promise you this. Once you have perfected this recipe, you will definitely be able to taste the difference between fresh made and boxed recipes. I warn you that it may make enjoying the fare offered by "international houses" (ahem!) that specialize in pancakes difficult.

A staple in my house, I make these at least once a week. Try adding dark chocolate chips or blueberries to the batter once in a while, too!

INGREDIENTS:

1 egg

1 $^1/_4$ cups buttermilk* (see NOTES for possible substitute)

$^1/_2$ tsp baking soda

1 $^1/_4$ cup flour (I use fresh ground soft white wheat)

1 tsp light brown sugar or honey (pure, raw, local honey is always best)

2 TBS grapeseed oil

1 tsp aluminum-free baking powder

$^1/_2$ tsp salt (Kosher or sea salt is best)

SUPPLIES:

measuring cups/spoons

mixing bowl

whisk

griddle or frying pan

PREPARATION:

Heat griddle or frying pan over medium to medium-high heat until you can feel the heat when you hold your hand above it. You don't want it too hot. Not high heat. If you drop a drop of water on it, the water should skitter along the surface. If you have a temperature gauge on your griddle, it should be set to about 375 to 400° degrees F (190.5° to 204° degrees C).

DIRECTIONS:

Beat the egg with the whisk. Add the buttermilk and baking soda. Mix well. Slowly add the remaining ingredients, whisking them in just until smooth.

Using a $1/4$ cup measuring cup, pour onto the griddle. Heat until the edges brown and bubbles form. Carefully flip over and cook just until the other side browns.

YIELD:

About 8 to 10 pancakes, depending on the size.

NUTRITION:

High in selenium

Nutrition Facts	
Serving Size 92 g	
Amount Per Serving	
Calories 170	Calories from Fat 54
	% Daily Value*
Total Fat 6.0g	9%
Saturated Fat 1.0g	5%
Cholesterol 29mg	10%
Sodium 363mg	15%
Total Carbohydrates 23.7g	8%
Dietary Fiber 0.7g	3%
Sugars 3.5g	
Protein 5.3g	
Vitamin A 1% • Vitamin C 1%	
Calcium 10% • Iron 8%	
* Based on a 2000 calorie diet	

NOTES:

Serve with real butter and maple syrup, honey, or molasses. You can also top with fresh fruit and freshly whipped cream.

Add $3/4$ cup fresh or frozen blueberries to the batter after it's mixed for blueberry pancakes.

Add one chopped banana and a dash of cinnamon for banana pancakes.

If the batter is too thick, add a little bit more buttermilk.

*If you don't have buttermilk, you can use regular whole milk with 1 TBS vinegar added to it. Let it sit for about 5 minutes before using. OR, use regular whole milk without the vinegar and increase baking powder by $1/2$ tsp and omit the baking soda.

SPICY PUMPKIN PANCAKES

I'm a big fan of squash. While the rest of the world celebrates a week of man eating sharks, I celebrate SQUASH WEEK on my website. I love winter squash pastries. These pancakes are no exception. They are spicy and delicious and the perfect compliment to a cold autumn morning.

INGREDIENTS:

2 eggs

1 cup buttermilk* (see NOTES for possible substitute)

1 cup pureed pumpkin (see NOTES)

1 $\frac{1}{2}$ cups flour (I use fresh ground soft white wheat)

1 tsp baking soda

2 tsp aluminum-free baking powder

1 tsp ground cinnamon

$\frac{1}{2}$ tsp ground ginger

$\frac{1}{2}$ tsp ground nutmeg

$\frac{1}{4}$ tsp salt

2 TBS grapeseed oil

1 tsp vanilla extract

2 TBS dark brown sugar or honey (pure, raw, local honey is always best)

SUPPLIES:

Measuring cups/spoons

whisk

bowl

griddle or frying pan

spatula

PREPARATION:

Heat griddle or frying pan over medium to medium-high heat until you can feel the heat when you hold your hand above it. You don't want it too hot. Not high heat. If you drop a drop of water on it, the water should skitter along the surface. If you have a temperature gauge on your griddle, it should be set to about 375° to 400° degrees F (190 ° to 205 ° degrees C).

DIRECTIONS:

Mix the dry ingredients. Add the wet ingredients and whisk just until mixed. If it's too thick, add a little more buttermilk.

Use a $^1/_4$ cup measuring cup to measure the batter onto the griddle or skillet.

Cook until the edges brown and bubbles form. Gently flip and cook until the other side is browned.

YIELD:

about 8 pancakes

NUTRITION:

Nutrition Facts

Serving Size 95 g

Amount Per Serving	
Calories 154	Calories from Fat 41
	% Daily Value*
Total Fat 4.6g	7%
Saturated Fat 0.8g	4%
Trans Fat 0.0g	
Cholesterol 37mg	12%
Sodium 250mg	10%
Total Carbohydrates 24.0g	8%
Dietary Fiber 1.9g	7%
Sugars 6.0g	
Protein 4.7g	
Vitamin A 68% •	Vitamin C 1%
Calcium 10% •	Iron 8%
* Based on a 2000 calorie diet	

High in selenium

Very high in vitamin A

NOTES:

Serve with maple syrup or apple butter.

I use fresh pumpkin. I cut the pumpkin in half, scoop out the seeds, and place each half flesh side down in a little bit of water in a pan. I bake them at about 375° degrees F (190° degrees C) until the flesh is soft enough to stick a fork through the skin easily. When they're cool enough to handle, I scoop out the flesh and freeze it in 1-cup increments. If you don't have fresh pumpkin on hand, you can use canned pumpkin – it just won't taste as good.

*No buttermilk? No problem. If you don't have buttermilk, you can use regular milk with 1 TBS vinegar added to it (let it sit for about 5 minutes before using). OR, use regular milk without the vinegar and increase baking powder by 1 tsp and omit baking soda from the recipe entirely.

EGGNOG PANCAKES

I set out with the intent of creating a week of "Christmas Breakfast Ideas" on my website and had the thought of doing an eggnog pancake recipe. Well, the eggnog recipe that I've been making since my mom would let me into the kitchen is simply this: 1 egg, 1 cup whole milk, sugar, and spices to taste.

Since my pancake recipe calls for 1 egg and 1 cup of milk already, rather than having to go through the extra bowl and beaters to make eggnog and add it in, I decided to just make pancakes with eggnog seasonings.

This recipe is not the same as my Family Favorite Buttermilk Pancakes. When you use buttermilk, you use less baking powder because it reacts with the baking soda to create leavening. Take this as a separate recipe because the measurements are different.

INGREDIENTS:

1 egg

1 cup whole milk

1 cup flour (I use fresh ground soft white wheat)

2 TBS melted unsalted butter

2 TBS sugar* (see NOTES)

1 TBS aluminum-free baking powder

$^{1}/_{2}$ TBS vanilla extract

$^{1}/_{2}$ tsp salt (Kosher or sea salt is best)

$^{1}/_{4}$ tsp fresh ground nutmeg

1 dash of cinnamon

SUPPLIES:

Measuring cups/spoons

bowl

whisk

griddle or frying pan

PREPARATION:

Melt butter. Heat griddle to 400° degrees F (204° degrees C). If using a skillet, heat it to just hotter than medium heat.

DIRECTIONS:

Beat the egg and milk with the whisk. Whisk in the remaining ingredients and whisk just until smooth.

I use a $1/4$ measuring cup – pour onto the griddle. Heat until the edges brown and bubbles form. Carefully flip over and cook just until the other side browns.

YIELD:

about 12 pancakes, depending on size

NUTRITION:

Nutrition Facts

Serving Size 98 g

Amount Per Serving

Calories 200	Calories from Fat 66
	% Daily Value*
Total Fat 7.4g	11%
Saturated Fat 4.2g	21%
Trans Fat 0.0g	
Cholesterol 50mg	17%
Sodium 300mg	13%
Total Carbohydrates 28.1g	9%
Dietary Fiber 0.8g	3%
Sugars 7.9g	
Protein 5.3g	
Vitamin A 5% •	Vitamin C 0%
Calcium 20% •	Iron 9%
* Based on a 2000 calorie diet	

High in phosphorus

High in selenium

NOTES:

Serve with real butter and maple syrup, honey, or molasses.

You can also top with fresh fruit and freshly whipped cream.

These are simply amazing topped with spiced apples.

*This recipe calls for sugar. You can substitute honey (local raw is best) instead in an equal or slightly lesser amount.

When I make these, I sometimes use vanilla sugar – that is sugar stored in an airtight container with a whole vanilla bean in it.

HEARTY WHOLE GRAIN WAFFLES

This is my go-to recipe for waffles in the hotel-style waffle maker. They have an amazing flavor and pack a nutritious punch that would be hard pressed to be beaten. I love serving them with real butter and real maple syrup or fresh organic berries.

INGREDIENTS:

1 $^1/_2$ cups whole wheat flour (I use fresh ground soft white wheat)

$^1/_2$ cup ground flax seeds

$^1/_8$ cup rolled oats

$^1/_4$ cup sunflower seeds

1 TBS aluminum-free baking powder

1 TBS brown sugar or honey (pure, raw, local honey is always best)

$^1/_2$ tsp salt (Kosher or sea salt is best)

1 $^1/_8$ cup whole milk

$^1/_8$ cup extra virgin coconut oil, melted

2 eggs

SUPPLIES:

bowl

whisk

measuring cups/spoons

waffle iron

PREPARATION:

Preheat waffle iron.

Melt coconut oil.

DIRECTIONS:

Mix dry ingredients. Add milk, coconut oil, and eggs. Mix just until moistened.

Follow the directions for your waffle iron.

YIELD:

4 servings

NUTRITION:

Nutrition Facts

Serving Size 102 g

Amount Per Serving	
Calories 252	Calories from Fat 100
	% Daily Value*
Total Fat 11.1g	17%
Saturated Fat 5.1g	26%
Cholesterol 51mg	17%
Sodium 206mg	9%
Total Carbohydrates 27.1g	9%
Dietary Fiber 5.3g	21%
Sugars 4.6g	
Protein 9.3g	

Vitamin A 2%	•	Vitamin C 0%
Calcium 18%	•	Iron 13%

* Based on a 2000 calorie diet

High in phosphorus

High in selenium

NOTES:

Sift dry ingredients to break the texture down some.

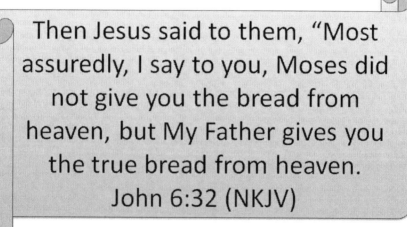

Then Jesus said to them, "Most assuredly, I say to you, Moses did not give you the bread from heaven, but My Father gives you the true bread from heaven.
John 6:32 (NKJV)

MA-MAW LUCILLE'S BUTTERMILK BISCUITS

My husband's great grandmother could whip these out by the dozen in about 20 minutes. They are the world's best biscuit. The original recipe called for vegetable shortening – I either use a trans-fat free vegetable shortening (organic palm shortening) or unsalted butter.

INGREDIENTS:

2 cups flour (I use fresh ground soft white wheat)

2 tsp aluminum-free baking powder

$^{1}/_{2}$ tsp baking soda

1 tsp salt

$^{1}/_{4}$ cup palm shortening or cold butter

$^{3}/_{4}$ cup buttermilk* (See NOTES for possible substitution)

SUPPLIES:

sifter

measuring cups/spoons

rolling pin and workspace

biscuit cutter (clean, dry large soup can or medium drinking cup also works)

cookie sheet or baking pan

PREPARATION:

Preheat oven to 500° degrees F (260° degrees C)

DIRECTIONS:

Sift together flour, baking powder, baking soda, and salt. Add shortening and cut in until mixture resembles fine crumbs. Blend in buttermilk to make the dough.

Put onto floured surface and roll until $^{1}/_{2}$ inch thick. Cut biscuits and place on greased pan.

Bake 8 to 10 minutes or until golden brown.

YIELD:

Makes about 12 biscuits.

NUTRITION:

Nutrition Facts	
Serving Size 84 g	
Amount Per Serving	
Calories 241	Calories from Fat 83
	% Daily Value*
Total Fat 9.2g	14%
Saturated Fat 4.3g	21%
Cholesterol 1mg	0%
Sodium 526mg	22%
Total Carbohydrates 34.0g	11%
Dietary Fiber 1.2g	5%
Sugars 1.6g	
Protein 5.3g	
Vitamin A 0% • Vitamin C 1%	
Calcium 11% • Iron 12%	
* Based on a 2000 calorie diet	

Very low in cholesterol

Low in sugar

NOTES:

The more often you make this recipe, the better you will become at judging the right consistency for the biscuit dough. They are wonderful with real butter, blackberry jam, molasses, or to "sop up" gravy.

*If you don't have buttermilk, you can use regular milk with 1 TBS vinegar added to it (let it sit for about 5 minutes before using).

QUICK CINNAMON ROLLS

Traditionally, cinnamon rolls use a yeast bread dough. This recipe uses Ma-Maw Lucille's Buttermilk Biscuits as a base, and gives you the opportunity to have sticky, delicious, hot, cinnamony goodness within half an hour of deciding you want to make a batch.

INGREDIENTS:

1 recipe Ma-Maw Lucille's Buttermilk Biscuits

3 TBS butter, softened

¼ cup brown sugar

1 TBS cinnamon

SUPPLIES:

Measuring cups/spoons

Knife

Rolling pin

Round cake pan

PREPARATION:

Preheat oven to 450° degrees F (230° degrees C)

Prepare the biscuit dough.

Grease the cake pan with butter.

DIRECTIONS:

Roll the dough out to a rectangle about $\frac{1}{8}$ inch thick.

Spread with the butter. Sprinkle with the brown sugar. Sprinkle with the cinnamon.

Roll from the long end. Cut into 12 equal pieces.

Place cut-side up in the cake pan. These are going to rise while baking, so don't overcrowd your pan.

Bake for 15 to 20 minutes, or until browned.

Invert onto a plate and serve.

YIELD:

Makes about 12 rolls.

NUTRITION:

Nutrition Facts

Serving Size 99 g

Amount Per Serving	
Calories 310	Calories from Fat 127
	% Daily Value*
Total Fat 14.1g	22%
Saturated Fat 8.7g	44%
Trans Fat 0.0g	
Cholesterol 37mg	12%
Sodium 623mg	26%
Total Carbohydrates 40.9g	14%
Dietary Fiber 1.8g	7%
Sugars 7.5g	
Protein 5.5g	

Vitamin A 9%	•	Vitamin C 1%
Calcium 13%	•	Iron 12%
* Based on a 2000 calorie diet		

High in Vitamin A

High in Iron

No Trans Fats

NOTES:

You can add raisins or nuts or both to the brown sugar. Sliced apples or even apple sauce would also be good!

CINNAMON HONEY SCONES WITH RAISINS

There is an online resource I visit often. I first found this delicious scone recipe by Wardeh "Wardee" Harmon on her website GNOWFGLINS.com which stands for God's natural, organic, whole foods, grown locally, in season.

This is a soaked wheat recipe – you soak the wheat overnight in an acidic liquid (in this case, apple cider vinegar) so that the phytic acid in the grain is broken down and your body is able to absorb ALL of the nutrients in the grain.

I made this recipe to take to Sunday School for breakfast. I worried that they would be heavy and dense. Far from it. They were amazing. They were so light, and melt-in-your-mouth. Enjoy.

INGREDIENTS:

2 ¹/₄ cups fresh ground soft white wheat flour

6 generous tsp extra virgin coconut oil

1 TBS apple cider vinegar

¹/₂ cup plus 2 TBS coconut milk

2 TBS honey (Pure, raw, local honey is always best)

1 ¹/₂ tsp ground cinnamon

¹/₂ tsp baking soda

1 ¹/₂ tsp aluminum-free baking powder

³/₄ tsp salt (Kosher or sea salt is best)

¹/₈ cup raisins

SUPPLIES:

large bowl

rolling pin

pizza cutter or sharp knife

measuring cups/spoons

baking sheet

PREPARATION:

Cut the coconut oil into the flour until the mixture resembles a bowl of crumbs. Add the coconut milk and the vinegar. Mix well.

Cover with a towel and set aside for **8** hours or overnight.

The next day, preheat the oven to 450° degrees F (230° degrees C).

Lightly oil baking sheet with coconut oil.

DIRECTIONS:

Gently mix in the honey, cinnamon, baking soda, baking powder, and salt.

Mix well. Add raisins.

Put on floured surface. Roll to $\frac{1}{2}$ thick.

Using a pizza cutter or a sharp knife, cut into 2 inch squares or 12 triangular wedges.

Place on cookie sheet. Bake 8 to 10 minutes.

YIELD:

About 12 scones

NUTRITION:

No cholesterol

Nutrition Facts

Serving Size 92 g

Amount Per Serving	
Calories 301	Calories from Fat 99

	% Daily Value*
Total Fat 11.0g	17%
Saturated Fat 9.5g	47%
Trans Fat 0.0g	
Cholesterol 0mg	0%
Sodium 401mg	17%
Total Carbohydrates 46.3g	15%
Dietary Fiber 2.3g	9%
Sugars 8.1g	
Protein 5.5g	

Vitamin A 0%	•	Vitamin C 1%	
Calcium 7%	•	Iron 16%	

* Based on a 2000 calorie diet

NOTES:

This is only slightly sweet. You can add more honey for more sweetness, just reduce the amount of coconut milk to accommodate the volume.

MARVELOUS MAPLE MUFFINS

The morning I created this recipe, my 5-year-old ate about 6 mini muffins before I managed to move them out of his reach. My teen aged daughter only ate one and left for school. When she came home, she said, "I have a confession to make. I didn't like those muffins."

It's rare for a member of my family to not like a recipe or to admit to not liking a recipe, and I guess she had to shore up her decision to tell me (which is silly, but I love her.) A few minutes later, I walked into the kitchen and she was shoving 2 mini muffins into her mouth while talking on a 3-way call with a couple of friends. She saw me and swallowed and said, "I love them with butter. Wow. These are so good!"

So, I guess the moral of that story is … serve them with real butter.

INGREDIENTS:

2 cups flour (I use fresh ground soft white wheat)

$^1/_4$ cup brown sugar or honey (Pure, raw, local honey is always best)

1 TBS aluminum-free baking powder

$^1/_2$ tsp salt (Kosher or sea salt is best)

$^1/_4$ cup coconut oil

1 egg

$^1/_2$ cup real maple syrup

$^1/_2$ cup whole milk

SUPPLIES:

bowl

whisk

wooden spoon

muffin tin

PREPARATION:

Either line the muffin tin with paper, or lightly grease it.

Preheat the oven to 400° degrees F (205° degrees C).

Melt the coconut oil.

DIRECTIONS:

Mix the dry ingredients.

Make a well in the middle and add the coconut oil, egg, syrup, and milk.

Using the whisk, whisk just until all of the wet ingredients and coconut oil are incorporated into the dry ingredients.

Fill the muffin cups ⅛ full. Bake 20 to 25 minutes or until golden brown. (I made mini-muffins and baked them for about 12 minutes.)

Serve with butter. ☺

YIELD:

12 muffins or 24 mini muffins

NUTRITION:

Nutrition Facts

Serving Size 92 g

Amount Per Serving	
Calories 276	Calories from Fat 75
	% Daily Value*
Total Fat 8.3g	13%
Saturated Fat 6.7g	33%
Cholesterol 22mg	7%
Sodium 165mg	7%
Total Carbohydrates 47.2g	16%
Dietary Fiber 0.9g	4%
Sugars 20.6g	
Protein 4.4g	

Vitamin A 1%	•	Vitamin C 0%
Calcium 12%	•	Iron 11%

* Based on a 2000 calorie diet

High in manganese

No Trans Fats

NOTES:

Do not use artificial syrup. You will not like the outcome.

Most artificial syrups are just flavored corn syrup or high fructose corn syrup or both and simply will not work with this recipe.

The good news is that you can use any grade of maple syrup. No need to use AAA. In fact, B may give your muffins a richer flavor and will save you some pennies at the market.

WHOLE WHEAT BLUEBERRY MUFFINS

I always have blueberries in the freezer for making smoothies, and all summer I keep fresh blueberries on hand in the refrigerator. About once a week, I make muffins for breakfast, and blueberry muffins are a family favorite.

INGREDIENTS:

2 cups flour (I use fresh ground soft white wheat)

$\frac{1}{4}$ cup raw sugar

1 TBS aluminum-free baking powder

$\frac{1}{2}$ tsp salt (Kosher or sea salt is best)

$\frac{1}{4}$ cup extra virgin coconut oil

1 egg

1 cup whole milk

1 cup fresh or frozen blueberries

SUPPLIES:

bowl

spoon

measuring cups/spoons

muffin tin

PREPARATION:

Melt the coconut oil.

Preheat oven to 400° degrees F (205° degrees C)

Grease muffin tin or line with liners.

DIRECTIONS:

Mix the dry ingredients. Add the coconut oil, egg, and milk. Mix just until mixed. Add blueberries. Gently stir until incorporated.

Spoon into muffin tin, filling each cup $\frac{1}{2}$ full.

Bake at 400° degrees F (205° degrees C) 20 to 25 minutes or until golden brown.

Remove from oven and immediately remove the muffins from the muffin tin.

YIELD:

12 muffins

NUTRITION:

High in Antioxidants

No Trans Fats

Nutrition Facts

Serving Size 101 g

Amount Per Serving	
Calories 238	Calories from Fat 79
	% Daily Value*
Total Fat 8.8g	14%
Saturated Fat 7.0g	35%
Cholesterol 24mg	8%
Sodium 170mg	7%
Total Carbohydrates 35.0g	12%
Dietary Fiber 1.3g	5%
Sugars 9.8g	
Protein 5.0g	

Vitamin A 1%	•	Vitamin C 3%
Calcium 12%	•	Iron 10%

* Based on a 2000 calorie diet

NOTES:

Recently, I mixed 2 TBS COLD butter, $^1/_3$ cup brown sugar, and $^1/_3$ cup rolled oats together and sprinkled that on top prior to baking for a streusel topping. It was REALLY delicious.

WHOLE WHEAT PUMPKIN CREAM CHEESE MUFFINS

This is the perfect recipe to make for a breakfast or brunch. They are packed with flavor from all of the spices, and the cream cheese is a beautifully decadent addition.

 INGREDIENTS:

3 cups flour (I use fresh ground soft white wheat)

1 tsp salt (Kosher or sea salt is best)

1 $^1/_4$ cups extra virgin coconut oil

2 cups pumpkin puree	2 TBS cocoa powder
$^1/_4$ cup unsulfured molasses	1 tsp baking soda
8 ounces cream cheese	4 tsp cinnamon
4 eggs	1 tsp ginger
2 cups raw sugar	2 tsp nutmeg
2 TBS powdered sugar	1 tsp ground cloves
$^1/_2$ tsp vanilla extract	$^1/_8$ tsp cardamom

$^1/_2$ cup chopped pumpkin seeds, walnuts, or pecans (optional)

 SUPPLIES:

Mixing bowl

measuring cups/spoons

2 12-well muffin tins

 PREPARATION:

Preheat oven to 350° degrees F (120° degrees C)

Grease muffin tin or line with paper cups.

Soften cream cheese. In a mixing bowl, blend it with powdered sugar and vanilla. Shape it into a log and place on a piece of waxed paper. Place in freezer for no more than an hour.

Melt the coconut oil.

DIRECTIONS:

Mix the flour, sugar, baking soda, cocoa, salt and spices.

Add the coconut oil, eggs, molasses, and pumpkin. Mix until just moistened.

Fill the muffin tins ¹/₂ full.

Remove the cream cheese from the freezer. Cut into 24 equal discs. Put a disc in the middle of each muffin, pressing down slightly. Sprinkle each muffin with 1 tsp chopped pumpkin seeds or nuts.

Bake at 350° degrees F (120° degrees C) for 20 to 25 minutes. Remove from oven and remove muffins from pan immediately.

YIELD:

24 muffins

NUTRITION:

Nutrition Facts	
Serving Size 105 g	
Amount Per Serving	
Calories 356	Calories from Fat 186
	% Daily Value*
Total Fat 20.6g	32%
Saturated Fat 15.6g	78%
Trans Fat 0.0g	
Cholesterol 45mg	15%
Sodium 228mg	9%
Total Carbohydrates 39.2g	13%
Dietary Fiber 1.9g	7%
Sugars 22.0g	
Protein 5.2g	
Vitamin A 80% •	Vitamin C 2%
Calcium 3% •	Iron 12%
* Based on a 2000 calorie diet	

Very high in vitamin A

NOTES:

Any winter squash will work in place of the pumpkin. Try butternut squash!

I use fresh pumpkin. I cut the pumpkin in half, scoop out the seeds, and place each half flesh side down in a little bit of water in a pan. I bake them at about 375° degrees F (190° degrees C) until the flesh is soft (I can stick a fork through the skin, even). When they're cool enough to handle, I scoop out the flesh and freeze it in 1-cup increments. But, if you don't have fresh pumpkin on hand, you can use canned pumpkin – it just won't taste as good.

OLD-FASHIONED CORNBREAD

It took me a few years, several brands of cornmeal, and many recipes to finally find one that everyone in my family loved. Now I have friends who ask for "Hallee's cornbread" and friends who come for dinner whose children want to know if they're having "Hallee's Special Cornbread!"

The cornmeal is the most essential ingredient. Since obtaining a grain mill, I grind organic popcorn and use it right away. If you have a mill I strongly recommend this. If not, and you aren't happy with your cornbread, try alternate brands of cornmeal until you hit upon the right one for you.

 INGREDIENTS:

1 cup yellow cornmeal (I once used only House Autry brand. Now I grind organic popcorn in my grain mill for fresh cornmeal.)

1 cup flour (I use fresh ground soft white wheat)

1 TBS honey (pure, raw, local honey is always best)

1 tsp salt (Kosher or sea salt is best)

1 TBS baking powder

2 eggs

1 $\frac{1}{4}$ cup whole milk

2 TBS oil (I don't recommend extra virgin olive oil in this case. Try grapeseed, safflower, or organic canola)

 SUPPLIES:

Measuring cups/spoons

mixing bowl

whisk

baking pan (I use 9 inch square pan or I also use cast-iron corn muffins pan)

 PREPARATION:

Heat oven to 425° degrees F (220° degrees C).

Grease pan.

DIRECTIONS:

Mix the dry ingredients. Make a well in the dry batter. Add the wet ingredients and mix, gently, with whisk until smooth. Pour into prepared pan.

Bake 15 to 20 minutes.

YIELD:

About 12 Servings

NUTRITION:

Nutrition Facts	
Serving Size 89 g	
Amount Per Serving	
Calories 191	Calories from Fat 59
	% Daily Value*
Total Fat 6.5g	10%
Saturated Fat 1.4g	7%
Trans Fat 0.0g	
Cholesterol 45mg	15%
Sodium 329mg	14%
Total Carbohydrates 28.5g	9%
Dietary Fiber 1.6g	6%
Sugars 4.2g	
Protein 5.5g	
Vitamin A 3% •	Vitamin C 0%
Calcium 13% •	Iron 9%
* Based on a 2000 calorie diet	

High in phosphorus

High in selenium

NOTES:

Serve warm with real butter and honey.

GREEK "PEASANT" CORNBREAD (BOBOTA)

In Greek, the word *bobota* can mean anything from cornmeal to any bread or polenta type dish made with cornmeal. In Greek history, during times of hardship, cornmeal recipes were very popular, and *bobota* is considered by many to be a "peasant" dish.

This recipe gets it's flavor from fresh orange juice and produces a dense, crumbly cornbread.

 INGREDIENTS:

2 cups yellow cornmeal (I once used only House Autry brand. Now I grind organic popcorn in my grain mill.)

$^{1}/_{4}$ cup honey (pure, raw, local honey is always best)

4 to 5 TBS fresh orange juice (juice of $^{1}/_{2}$ large orange)

$^{1}/_{4}$ cup extra virgin olive oil

1 cup lukewarm water

1 $^{1}/_{4}$ tsp aluminum-free baking powder –OR– 1 $^{1}/_{4}$ tsp baking soda* 9See NOTES)

 SUPPLIES:

Bowl/whisk for dry ingredients

Small bowl for wet ingredients

Measuring cups/spoons

9-inch pie plate

 PREPARATION:

Grease the pie plate.

Preheat oven to 350° degrees F (180° degrees C)

 DIRECTIONS:

Whisk together the cornmeal, baking powder to combine well. In a separate bowl, mix oil, honey, orange juice, and water, and stir until well blended. Add liquids to the dry ingredients and stir just until mixed.

Pour batter into a well-oiled 9-inch pie pan and bake at 350° degrees F (180° degrees C) for 40to 45 minutes. Test for doneness by inserting a toothpick into the center of the pan. It should come out dry.

Cool at least 10 minutes before cutting. Serve warm or at room temperature.

YIELD:

One 9-inch pie pan (4 to 8 pieces) of simple country cornbread

NUTRITION:

Nutrition Facts

Serving Size 86 g

Amount Per Serving	
Calories 199	Calories from Fat 67
	% Daily Value*
Total Fat 7.4g	11%
Saturated Fat 1.1g	5%
Cholesterol 0mg	0%
Sodium 12mg	1%
Total Carbohydrates 33.1g	11%
Dietary Fiber 2.3g	9%
Sugars 8.8g	
Protein 2.5g	
Vitamin A 2% •	Vitamin C 6%
Calcium 4% •	Iron 6%
* Based on a 2000 calorie diet	

No cholesterol

Very low in sodium

NOTES:

In Greek: pronounced bo-BOH-tah

This recipe sizes very well. To increase the yield, increase all ingredients proportionately.

Cornmeal is the most essential ingredient to any cornbread. Many factors will affect your cornbread from your altitude to the water table in your region but the cornmeal is the vital factor. Since obtaining a grain mill, I grind organic popcorn and use the resulting meal right away. If you have a mill I strongly recommend this. If not, and you aren't happy with your cornbread, try alternate brands of cornmeal until you hit upon the right one for you.

*Baking powder is double-acting, meaning that it causes a rise during preparation and again during baking. Baking soda causes a one-time rise. The *bobota* will reflect a slight difference, depending on which is used.

GRANDMA POE'S ZUCCHINI BREAD

This is my paternal grandmother's recipe – she gave it to my mother before I was born. An old Kentucky boy called this "the best zucchini bread he ever did eat." High compliments indeed.

INGREDIENTS:

3 cups flour (I use fresh ground soft white wheat)

3 eggs

2 ¹/₂ cups sugar

1 cup organic canola or safflower oil

3 tsp vanilla extract

2 cups grated fresh, unpeeled zucchini

3 tsp cinnamon

1 tsp baking soda

¹/₂ tsp aluminum-free baking powder

1 cup chopped nuts (optional) (I prefer pecans)

SUPPLIES:

Large bowl

measuring cups/spoons

Cheese grater

2 bread pans

pan of water

PREPARATION:

Preheat oven to 350° degrees F (180° degrees C).

Place a pan of water in the oven.

Grease and flour bread pans.

Grate the zucchini

DIRECTIONS:

Stir together eggs, sugar, oil, vanilla, and zucchini.

Sift together flour, salt, baking soda, baking powder, and cinnamon.

Mix into the wet ingredients. Add nuts.

Pour into two (2) bread pans.

Bake 350° degrees F (180° degrees C) for one hour.

YIELD:

Makes 2 loaves

NUTRITION:

Nutrition Facts

Serving Size 99 g

Amount Per Serving

Calories 391	Calories from Fat 176
	% Daily Value*
Total Fat 19.6g	30%
Saturated Fat 1.6g	8%
Trans Fat 0.0g	
Cholesterol 31mg	10%
Sodium 93mg	4%
Total Carbohydrates 51.1g	17%
Dietary Fiber 1.7g	7%
Sugars 32.0g	
Protein 4.3g	

Vitamin A 1%	•	Vitamin C 4%
Calcium 3%	•	Iron 8%

* Based on a 2000 calorie diet

Low in saturated fat

Low in sodium

NOTES:

I use extra virgin olive oil a lot but I do not like to use olive oil in my baking – I've never liked the taste. But a lot of people prefer the health benefits of olive oil over canola or safflower oil. Olive oil would work in this recipe just fine.

SHANNON'S BEAUTIFUL BANANA BREAD

I met a woman on a message board about four years ago. She posted this recipe, titling the post, "The Best Banana Bread You'll Ever Eat."

She wasn't exaggerating.

Nearly eight years later, all us women from that message board still talk about the banana bread. It really is the best banana bread you'll ever eat.

INGREDIENTS:

2 cups flour (I use fresh ground soft white wheat)

1 tsp aluminum-free baking powder

$^1/_2$ tsp salt (Kosher or sea salt is best)

1 tsp ground cinnamon

1 whole stick (room temperature) butter (no substitutions)

1 cup sugar

2 eggs (room temperature)

1 tsp vanilla extract

3 medium/large bananas, mashed

$^1/_2$ cup plain yogurt or sour cream

$^1/_2$ cup chopped nuts (optional – pecans or walnuts)

SUPPLIES:

Something with which to mash bananas. These days I use a potato masher. I've also used a food processor before.

large mixing bowl	bread pan
two smaller mixing bowls	parchment paper
sifter	wooden spoon
mixer	wire cooling rack

PREPARATION:

Line the bread pan with parchment paper. This will keep your loaf pan clean, and it will make it really easy to remove the bread. You can grease and flour it if you'd rather.

Heat oven to 325° degrees F (160° degrees C).

Mash bananas.

DIRECTIONS:

In a small bowl combine and sift dry ingredients: flour, powders, soda, cinnamon, salt. Set aside.

In the mixer bowl cream butter and sugar until fluffy. Add eggs one at a time.

In another bowl mix the mashed bananas Stir in the yogurt.

Using a wooden spoon, blend $1/4$ of dry ingredients into the butter mix. Then add $1/4$ of the banana mix into the butter mix. Keep doing this until both dry ingredients and banana mixture are gone. Add the nuts. Give a good quick stir, trying not to handle or stir the batter too much. Scrape batter into loaf pan and smooth top with the spoon.

Bake in center of oven at 325° degrees F (160° degrees C) for 70 to 75 minutes or until a knife inserted in the center comes out clean. Cool for a few minutes then remove from pan and finish cooling on a wire cooling rack.

NUTRITION:

Nutrition Facts	
Serving Size 100 g	
Amount Per Serving	
Calories 285	Calories from Fat 108
	% Daily Value*
Total Fat 12.0g	19%
Saturated Fat 5.5g	28%
Trans Fat 0.0g	
Cholesterol 48mg	16%
Sodium 170mg	7%
Total Carbohydrates 41.1g	14%
Dietary Fiber 1.9g	7%
Sugars 21.3g	
Protein 4.5g	
Vitamin A 6% •	Vitamin C 5%
Calcium 5% •	Iron 8%
* Based on a 2000 calorie diet	

Low in sodium

No Trans Fats

YIELD:

1 8x4x3 inch loaf

NOTES:

Also will make 4 miniature loaves. When my husband was deployed a popped mini-loaves into my Seal-a-meal and though dense, they kept for the journey and were a hit among the soldiers.

HEALTHY, THRIFTY HOMEMADE CRACKERS

Provided you aren't making cheese-crackers, homemade crackers are Daniel Fast friendly, Orthodox Fast friendly, and of course suitable for Lent. You can make crackers using different types of cooking surface, using many diverse kinds of grain, adding various seasonings if you like, and in just about any kind of shape you want, too.

Best of all, they are really easy to make.

Traditionally, crackers were baked in stone or brick ovens so if you have an oven stone, like a pizza stone, you can get fairly close to an artisan style cracker. They also cook up just fine on an ordinary cookie sheet.

For grains, I prefer fresh milled whole wheat flour, but just about any flour will do. Use cornmeal, buckwheat or other non-gluten grains for gluten free crackers.

This recipe makes a semi-crisp, fairly dense cracker.

INGREDIENTS:

1 ¼ cups whole wheat flour (I use fresh ground soft white wheat) (or substitute rye, buckwheat, spelt, cornmeal, etc.)

4 TBS (add more as needed) water

2 TBS (add more as needed) unsalted butter or extra virgin olive oil

½ tsp salt (Kosher or sea salt is best) or to taste

1 tsp seasoning or dried herb of your choice (optional)

SUPPLIES:

Food processor

Measuring cups/spoons

Sifter

Parchment paper

Rolling pin

Baking sheet or cooking stone

PREPARATION:

Preheat oven to 400° degrees F (205° degrees C)

Sift your flour to ensure a light cracker

DIRECTIONS:

In a food processor, mix 1 cup of flour, $\frac{1}{2}$ teaspoon salt and oil. Add 3 tablespoons water and mix well.

Gradually add more water, mixing after each addition, until mixture forms a compact ball. If it seems too sticky to handle, add a touch more flour and pulse. If it is too dry, sprinkle a little more water and pulse. Various factors, like altitude and humidity, affect this so use your good judgment.

Sprinkle your work surface (or parchment paper) with some of the remaining flour.

To prevent sticking, dust your hands and the rolling pin with a little more flour.

Press and roll the dough to about $\frac{1}{8}$ inch thickness. If the dough is too dry to roll out, return it to the food processor and add a little more water.

Try to get the dough really uniform. Setting two $\frac{1}{8}$ inch thick wooden dowels on either side of the dough so that the rolling pin eventually rides over the top of the dowels like rails is a good trick.

Place the rolled-out dough on a baking sheet (or cooking stone) dusted with a little flour or cornmeal. If you've used parchment paper, transfer dough and parchment paper directly to baking sheet.

If you like, take a serrated edge and press serrations into the dough; squares, rectangles, triangles, or whatever. This will result in perforations in the finished product. That will facilitate you being able to break the cracker sheet into crackers more easily upon completion.

TIP: A clean hair comb works great for this. (I have a comb that is only used for crackers – it stays with my baking supplies)

Place in preheated oven and bake at 400° degrees F (205° degrees C) for 10 to 15 minutes, until light brown.

Let cool on a wire rack and break into pieces.

If making several batches, mix another while the first one bakes. Remember that you can reuse the parchment paper several times.

YIELD:

About 1 pound of crackers

NUTRITION:

Nutrition Facts

Serving Size 83 g

Amount Per Serving

Calories 270	Calories from Fat 89
	% Daily Value*
Total Fat 9.8g	15%
Saturated Fat 1.4g	7%
Cholesterol 0mg	0%
Sodium 389mg	16%
Total Carbohydrates 39.8g	13%
Dietary Fiber 1.4g	6%
Protein 5.4g	
Vitamin A 1% •	Vitamin C 1%
Calcium 1% •	Iron 14%
* Based on a 2000 calorie diet	

Very low in sugar

No cholesterol

High in selenium

High in thiamin

NOTES:

Feel free to experiment with the herbs and seasonings if you don't want just a plain cracker. Some successful combinations might be cornmeal with chili powder, rye with caraway or dill seed, whole wheat with garlic powder, or spelt with poppy or sesame seed.

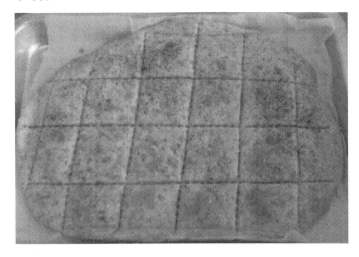

DELICIOUS CRANBERRY NUT BREAD

I make this bread in mini-loaf pans and give it as a gift during Christmas. It's a wonderful bread, the perfect balance between sweet and light.

INGREDIENTS:

2 cups flour (I use fresh ground soft white wheat)

1 cup sugar

1 $\frac{1}{2}$ tsp aluminum-free baking powder

1 tsp salt (Kosher or sea salt is best)

$\frac{1}{2}$ tsp baking soda

$\frac{1}{4}$ cup unsalted butter (cold)

1 egg

$\frac{3}{4}$ cup fresh squeezed orange juice

1 TBS grated orange peel (orange zest)

1 $\frac{1}{2}$ cups fresh cranberries

$\frac{1}{2}$ cup chopped nuts (walnuts or pecans)

SUPPLIES:

measuring cups/spoons

zester

juicer

1 large bowl

1 small bowl

pastry cutter or fork for cutting the butter into the flour

loaf pan

sharp knife and cutting board or a food processor

PREPARATION:

Zest the orange peel until you have 1 TBS

Squeeze the orange until you have $\frac{3}{4}$ cup

Chop the cranberries (I use a food processor)

Grease and flour loaf pan

Preheat oven to 350° degrees F (180° degrees C)

DIRECTIONS:

In the large bowl, combine flour, sugar, baking powder, baking soda, and salt. Using a fork or a pastry cutter, cut in butter until mixture resembles coarse crumbs.

In the small bowl, beat together the egg, orange juice, and orange peel.

Make a well in the center of the dry ingredients. Pour the egg mixture into the well, Gently stir just until blended. Add the cranberries and nuts.

Spoon into loaf pan and bake at 350° degrees F (180° degrees C) for 65 to 70 minutes or until a toothpick inserted near the center comes out clean. Cool in pan 10 minutes before removing from pan and cooling completely on a wire cooling rack.

NUTRITION:

Nutrition Facts

Serving Size 96 g

Amount Per Serving	
Calories 269	Calories from Fat 83
	% Daily Value*
Total Fat 9.2g	14%
Saturated Fat 3.4g	17%
Cholesterol 29mg	10%
Sodium 336mg	14%
Total Carbohydrates 44.0g	15%
Dietary Fiber 2.0g	8%
Sugars 22.4g	
Protein 3.9g	

Vitamin A 4%	•	Vitamin C 20%
Calcium 5%	•	Iron 8%

* Based on a 2000 calorie diet

High in vitamin C

No Trans Fats

YIELD:

1 8x4x2 inch loaf

–OR–

4 miniature loaves

NOTES:

Wonderful as a gift or to grace any dessert table over the holidays.

INDIAN FLAT BREAD

Chapattis are similar to tortillas, but made with no baking powder. They are easy to make and keep well if stored in an airtight container. Chapattis are common in Southeast Asia and throughout Africa.

INGREDIENTS:

2 ½ cups flour (I use fresh ground, soft white wheat)

2 cups water (or enough to make a soft dough)

1 pinch salt (Kosher or sea salt is best)

SUPPLIES:

Bowl

Rolling pin

Cast iron skillet

DIRECTIONS:

Mix flour and salt in a large mixing bowl.

Make a hole in flour and using your hand, mix in water to make a soft dough.

Knead for five minutes, return to the bowl, cover with wet cloth and refrigerate for an hour.

Heat a cast iron skillet over medium high heat until very hot.

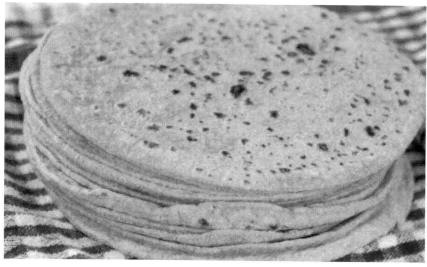

Roll out a small ball of dough into a flat round shape and place in pan, cooking for 1 minute on each side. Once turned press gently with a towel, until brown.

Repeat until all dough is used.

YIELD:

About 10 chapattis

NUTRITION:

Nutrition Facts	
Serving Size 98 g	
Amount Per Serving	
Calories 142	Calories from Fat 3
	% Daily Value*
Total Fat 0.4g	1%
Cholesterol 0mg	0%
Sodium 22mg	1%
Total Carbohydrates 29.8g	10%
Dietary Fiber 1.1g	4%
Protein 4.0g	
Vitamin A 0% •	Vitamin C 0%
Calcium 1% •	Iron 10%
* Based on a 2000 calorie diet	

Very low in saturated fat

No cholesterol

Very low in sodium

Very low in sugar

High in selenium

High in thiamin

NOTES:

If you wrap these in foil when they're warm, they should stay relatively soft until you're finished cooking the whole batch.

> But He answered and said, "It is written, 'Man shall not live by bread alone, but by every word that proceeds from the mouth of God.'"
> Matthew 4:4 (NKJV)

WHITE CORN TORTILLAS

One day, browsing through the kitchen store, my husband convinced me that our kitchen was incomplete without a tortilla press. Considering what huge fans we are of any kind of Mexican cuisine, it wasn't a hard sell.

I had it in my gadgets drawer for several months before I remembered to buy the right kind of flour and follow the directions. I cannot tell you how much my family enjoys using these tortillas when we have tacos or enchiladas. They taste wonderful, and you can have the comfort in knowing that they weren't made in a factory months ago, but that they were made fresh and hot in your kitchen with exactly 3 ingredients.

 INGREDIENTS:

2 cups organic corn masa flour

$^1/_4$ tsp salt (Kosher or sea salt is best)

1 $^1/_4$ cup water

 SUPPLIES:

measuring cups/spoons

bowl

tortilla press or a rolling pin

waxed paper

 DIRECTIONS:

Mix all of the ingredients together. I stir with a spoon just to get the flour wet, then use my hand.

Break the dough into 16 equal parts. Cover with a damp paper towel.

Line the tortilla press with waxed paper.

Place one of the balls of dough in the middle, cover with waxed paper, and press down to form the tortilla.

Heat a skillet kind of hot. Place the tortilla on it. Cook until it starts to brown, then flip it and cook the other side.

I have a tortilla keeper that I line with foil and place them in as I cook them. This keeps them warm. You can line a bowl with foil and do the same thing, just recover them with the foil as you add to them.

YIELD:

16 tortillas

NUTRITION:

Nutrition Facts

Serving Size 88 g

Amount Per Serving	
Calories 139	Calories from Fat 13

	% Daily Value*
Total Fat 1.4g	2%
Cholesterol 0mg	0%
Sodium 100mg	4%
Total Carbohydrates 29.0g	10%
Dietary Fiber 3.6g	15%
Protein 3.5g	

Vitamin A 0%	•	Vitamin C 0%
Calcium 6%	•	Iron 15%

* Based on a 2000 calorie diet

Very high in thiamin

High in riboflavin

High in niacin

High in iron

High in dietary fiber

Low in saturated fat

Very low in sugar

No cholesterol

NOTES:

We have handy taco-holders that we use when we're making tacos, because the tortillas are not formed in the bent shape. This allows us to load our tacos and keep them ready to go until we pick them up to eat them.

If you want a thinner tortilla (like for enchiladas), once you've pressed it you can put it between two pieces of waxed paper and roll it out more. Also, if you don't have a tortilla press, you can use the same method to roll them out to begin with.

WHOLE WHEAT FLOUR TORTILLAS

These are so delicious. It's hard to keep my kids out of them while I'm making them. I have a tortilla press that I use to make them. Before I owned it, I rolled my tortillas out with a rolling pin. The tortilla press cooks and flattens at the same time -and makes making tortillas SO easy. If you want to have homemade tortillas on hand regularly, I'd highly recommend a press.

INGREDIENTS:

2 to 3 cups flour (I use fresh ground soft white wheat)

1 cup warm water

$^{1}/_{4}$ cup extra virgin olive oil

1 tsp salt (Kosher or sea salt is best)

SUPPLIES:

medium bowl

rolling pin

skillet or griddle

wax paper

DIRECTIONS:

Combine the water, olive oil, and salt. Add the flour until the dough comes together and is soft but not sticky. You may not need all 3 cups.

Let rest for 20 minutes.

Divide into 8 equal portions. Roll each piece of dough into a ball.

On a lightly floured surface, use a rolling pin to flatten each ball into an 8-inch or 10-inch circle. The tortilla will be very thin. Stack between pieces of waxed paper.

Place a tortilla on a medium-hot ungreased skillet or griddle.

Cook about 30 seconds or until the dough starts to puff and bubble up.

Turn and cook another 30 seconds.

Place in a tortilla holder or wrap in foil. This will keep it moist and soft.

YIELD:

8 10-inch tortillas

NUTRITION:

Nutrition Facts

Serving Size 112 g

Amount Per Serving	
Calories 300	Calories from Fat 81

	% Daily Value*
Total Fat 9.0g	14%
Saturated Fat 1.3g	7%
Cholesterol 0mg	0%
Sodium 390mg	16%
Total Carbohydrates 47.7g	16%
Dietary Fiber 1.7g	7%
Protein 6.5g	

Vitamin A 0%	•	Vitamin C 0%
Calcium 1%	•	Iron 16%

* Based on a 2000 calorie diet

High in selenium

High in thiamin

Low in saturated fat

Very low in sugar

No cholesterol

NOTES:

To freeze, stack in between waxed paper and place in a freezer bag or wrap tightly with foil. Thaw completely before use.

These are perfect for quesadillas, tacos, burritos. I can't wait to try out chimichangas or to make my own tortillas chips!

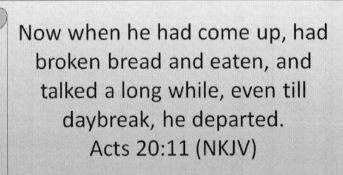

Now when he had come up, had broken bread and eaten, and talked a long while, even till daybreak, he departed.
Acts 20:11 (NKJV)

TRADITIONAL CHICKEN TAMALES

You my wonder why a tamales is a recipe in a bread cookbook. I decided tamales are really just stuffed cornbread, so, I'm including it in my bread cookbook. You'll love this recipe so much I know you'll be glad I did.

My husband judges Mexican restaurants by the quality of their tamales. If they aren't hand made, steamed in a corn husk, with the right favors he simply won't go back to that restaurant. Consequently, it took me several years to even attempt a recipe for tamales. I was so excited to find one that he loves.

INGREDIENTS:

6-8 chicken thighs

Salt to taste (Kosher or sea salt is best)

fresh ground black pepper to taste

2 $1/4$ cups Masa Harina tortilla flour

1 cup warm water

$3/4$ cup palm shortening

$1/4$ tsp salt (Kosher or sea salt is best)

$1/4$ cup chili powder

2 TBS extra virgin olive oil

1 (14 $1/2$ ounce) can tomatoes

2 cloves of garlic

2 tsp honey (pure, raw, local honey is always best)

$1/2$ tsp oregano

$1/2$ tsp cumin

15 to 18 corn husks

SUPPLIES:

baking sheet for chicken

measuring cups/spoons

Saucepan

steamer pan

Bowl

blender/mixer

PREPARATION:

Soak the corn husks in water for several hours. I put them in a large bowl, cover them with filtered water, then put another bowl filled with water on top so that it is weighted down and forces all of them under the water.

Place chicken on pan. Salt and pepper to taste. Bake at 375° degrees F (190° degrees C) for about 20 to 25 minutes or until cooked through. Let them cool, then remove the chicken from the bones and finely chop.

Mix the tortilla flour and shortening. Cover. Let stand for 20 minutes.

DIRECTIONS:

While the tortilla flour and water and sitting, place extra virgin olive oil in small saucepan and heat over medium-low heat. Once hot, add the chili powder. Cook for 4 minutes.

In a blender, put can of undrained tomatoes, garlic, seasoning. Add chili powder and extra virgin olive oil mixture. Blend until smooth.

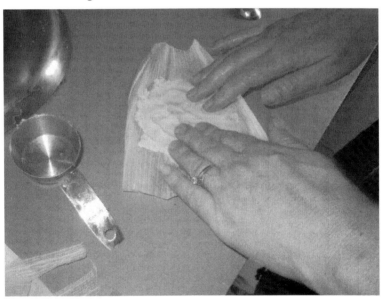

Return to the saucepan and bring to a boil. Reduce heat and simmer, uncovered, for 10 minutes. Sauce will thicken.

Put tortilla flour/water mixture in mixer bowl. Add salt and shortening. Beat at medium speed until well combined.

Before rolling up your tamales, fill your steamer pan with water and start heating it. Bring it to a boil and reduce the heat to medium heat. Take a corn husk and pat it dry with a paper towel. Place $\frac{1}{4}$ cup dough mixture on the tortilla.

Pat out flat, leaving edges of corn husk clear.

Top with 1 Tablespoon chili sauce and 1 Tablespoon chicken. Tightly roll the corn husk.

Tie ends. I use a corn husk that I've ripped into strips.

Place in steamer basket.

Once all tamales have been rolled, steam in steamer basket for 35 minutes over medium heat. Serve with chili sauce.

NUTRITION:

Nutrition Facts	
Serving Size 112 g	
Amount Per Serving	
Calories 219	Calories from Fat 104
	% Daily Value*
Total Fat 11.5g	18%
Saturated Fat 4.4g	22%
Cholesterol 42mg	14%
Sodium 83mg	3%
Total Carbohydrates 11.8g	4%
Dietary Fiber 1.7g	7%
Sugars 1.2g	
Protein 17.7g	
Vitamin A 10% •	Vitamin C 9%
Calcium 3% •	Iron 11%
* Based on a 2000 calorie diet	

Very high in vitamin B6

High in niacin

Low in sodium

Low in sugar

YIELD:

12 to 15 tamales

NOTES:

I am not able to find corn husks in every store. If you keep a garden, you can use your own corn husks. Just dry wash them and hang them on a thread to dry out for a few months or put them in a dehydrator.

You can find corn husks at just about any Hispanic grocers and I almost always find them in the Hispanic sections of the ethnic food aisle of any commissary if you have on post access to a military base. One place I have always found them is Walmart.

I can't recommend using regular cornmeal as a substitute for the Masa Harina tortilla flour. I have tried several different ways and it just never works out. I recommend just using the Masa flour. You can find it in most grocery stores. If it's not in the baking aisle, check the ethnic foods aisle in the Hispanic foods section.

EASY CHEESEY CHILI EMPTANADITAS

This is an amazing dish. The pastry is so light and buttery that it nearly melts in your mouth. The cheese combined with the chilies is a remarkable flavor. They can be an appetizer for a *Cinco de Mayo* celebration, or a delicious and savory treat for lunch.

 INGREDIENTS:

2 cups flour (I used fresh ground soft white wheat)

1 tsp salt (Kosher or sea salt is best)

10 TBS cold unsalted butter (that's $^1/_2$ cup plus 2 TBS)

5 to 6 TBS cold water

$^3/_4$ cup shredded Havarti cheese with jalepeno peppers

1 7-ounce can diced green chilies

1 egg

1 TBS water

chili powder to taste

 SUPPLIES:

2 bowls

pastry cutter or fork

spoon

pastry brush

baking sheet

 PREPARATION:

Preheat oven to 400° degrees F (205° degrees C)

Shred cheese.

 DIRECTIONS:

Mix together the cheese and the diced green chilies. Set aside.

Mix flour and salt. Cut butter into flour mixture until it resembles fine crumbs. Add water and stir, starting with 4 TBS and then adding one TBS at a time just until a ball of dough forms.

Put on floured surface.

You have two options for the next few steps.:

OPTION ONE: I have a turnover maker tool – so, if you have a similar tool, follow these instructions:

Roll out to about a 12-inch circle, about the same thickness as a pie crust. Using a 3-inch turnover tool, cut out a circle. Place dough on tool.

Spoon 1 tsp chili/cheese mixture onto the center of the dough. Brush edge with water. Fold over and seal. Place on ungreased baking sheet.

OPTION TWO: Rolling by hand:

Take a ball of dough about the size of a large gum ball. Roll it into a 3-inch circle. Place 1 tsp chili/cheese mixture in the center of the dough. Brush edge with water. Fold the dough over. Crimp the edges with a fork. Place on an ungreased baking sheet. Lightly beat egg and 1 TBS water.

Brush empanaditas with egg. Sprinkle with chili powder.

Bake in 400° degrees F (205° degrees C) oven for 13 minutes or until nicely browned.

Serve with sour cream.

YIELD:

16 to 18, depending on how you roll your dough

NUTRITION:

Nutrition Facts	
Serving Size 109 g	
Amount Per Serving	
Calories 399	Calories from Fat 202
	% Daily Value*
Total Fat 22.4g	34%
Saturated Fat 13.3g	67%
Cholesterol 78mg	26%
Sodium 532mg	22%
Total Carbohydrates 41.9g	14%
Dietary Fiber 8.0g	32%
Sugars 10.9g	
Protein 11.1g	
Vitamin A 145% •	Vitamin C 13%
Calcium 15% •	Iron 17%
* Based on a 2000 calorie diet	

Very high in vitamin A

NOTES:

Pepper Jack cheese can be used as a substitute for the Havarti.

FRIED BREAD

Oh yes. You heard that correctly. Fried bits of bread dough. Some sprinkled with sugar, some drizzled with honey, some dusted with chili powder. All fried to golden, crisp perfection. Enjoy. I know I do.

GREEK LENTEN FRITTERS (TIGANITES)

Similar to small pancakes, these light, crispy medallion-sized treats are a delight served with honey or *petimezi* (a kind of traditional grape syrup) ... or with any syrup for that matter.

Try them with preserves, jams, jellies, or a creative topping of your own design. They can be eaten as a sweet snack, with breakfast, or as a brunch dish.

INGREDIENTS:

2 bottles of organic ginger ale or ginger brew

1 cup pure water

2 tsp of any of several anise, star anise, or licorice flavored liqueur or brandy such as *ouzo* or *raki** (see NOTES for suggestions and/or substitutes) –OR– finely ground aniseed to taste

2 TBS lemon juice

4 $\frac{1}{2}$ cups flour (I use fresh ground soft white wheat)

1 tsp salt (Kosher or sea salt is always best)

3 tsp aluminum-free baking powder

Extra virgin coconut oil for frying

Serve with honey (pure, raw, local honey is always best), *petimezi*, real syrups, or your favorite jellies, jams, or preserves

SUPPLIES:

bowl

mixer

sifter

frying pan

measuring cups/spoons

metal slotted spoon

paper towels

PREPARATION:

Preheat $\frac{1}{8}$ inch to $\frac{1}{4}$ inch of extra virgin coconut oil in frying pan over medium-high heat.

DIRECTIONS:

Using an electric mixer, beat the ginger ale, salt, water, liqueur, and lemon juice on low speed. Sift together the baking powder and flour and add slowly to the bowl, beating on high.

When all the flour has been added, continue to beat on high speed for 2 to 3 minutes until smooth.

Preheat $\frac{1}{8}$ inch to $\frac{1}{4}$ inch of coconut oil in a heavy-bottomed frying pan or skillet over medium-high heat. When hot, fry the pancakes using a rounded tablespoon of batter for each. Fry 2 to 3 minutes on each side until lightly golden.

Remove from pan with a metal slotted spoon. Drain well on paper towels.

Add more oil between batches if the level in the pan drops too low.

NUTRITION:

Nutrition Facts

Serving Size 114 g

Amount Per Serving	
Calories 167	Calories from Fat 4
	% Daily Value*
Total Fat 0.4g	1%
Cholesterol 0mg	0%
Sodium 173mg	7%
Total Carbohydrates 35.8g	12%
Dietary Fiber 1.1g	4%
Sugars 4.7g	
Protein 4.2g	

Vitamin A 0%	•	Vitamin C 2%
Calcium 5%	•	Iron 11%

* Based on a 2000 calorie diet

High in selenium

High in thiamin

Very low in saturated fat

YIELD:

Approximately 10 servings of 4 to 5 pancakes each

NOTES:

In Greek: pronounced tee-ghah-NEE-tess

*About the liqueur element of this recipe: Personally, though I am not exactly well known for my fondness for distilled liquor, I have no objection to cooking with alcohol or alcohol based extracts. I live in Kentucky the birthplace of *bourbon whisky* and *corn moonshine*. There is even an annual phenomenon known as the Kentucky Derby which seems to bring people to the conclusion that a concoction referred to as a *mint julip* is a good thing.

Unless one is purposeful about preserving the alcohol as in *bourbon balls* or *mint julip candy* (shudder), the majority of the alcohol burns off or evaporates by the time a recipe reaches my table.

So, I may use a dollop of *wine* to get the most out of a bone broth or a bottle of *beer* to batter my onion rings or a tablespoon of *vanilla extract* to flavor my desserts. The key is that I use alcohol as an ingredient that enhances flavor and not as the main course.

For the alcohol related portion of this recipe, essentially what you want to end up with is that subtle hint of a licorice flavor permeating the fritters. Traditionally, these recipes call for any of the category of liqueurs flavored with either anise, star anise, or licorice. There are many hundreds of these liqueurs going back centuries and include anything from *ouzo* to *absinthe* so if there is a regional preference, just about any will do.

Examples include *anisette* and *pastis* from France, *ouzo* and *mistra* from Greece, *anesone* and *sambuca* from Italy, *anis* and *ojen* from Spain, *raki* and *arraki* from Turkey, and *kasra* from Libya.

For this recipe, you can obtain a similar flavor without alcohol. Basically, you want that subtle anise or licorice flavor. Substitutes can include: aniseed (finely ground) OR anise extract (Substitute a teaspoon of anise extract for every 1 or 2 tablespoons liqueur.)

GREEK LENTEN TOMATO FRITTERS (DOMATOKEFTETHES)

Tomato fritters are a delightful appetizer or side dish, and a specialty of Santorini, a Greek island known for its tomatoes. The combination of herbs can be adjusted to include dill, parsley, basil, mint, or oregano, depending on taste preference. This meatless, eggless, dairyless dish is perfect for Lent or a Daniel Fast. The fresh vegetables in it also make a wonderful summer dish to prepare with the bounty out of a vegetable garden (and, come on – who isn't desperately searching for zucchini recipes right around mid-August?)

 INGREDIENTS:

2 cups flour (I use fresh ground soft white wheat)

2 tsp aluminum-free baking powder

4 ripe medium tomatoes

2 medium zucchini

1 medium onion

$^3/_4$ cup fresh parsley

$^3/_4$ cup fresh mint or fresh basil, finely chopped

1 tsp salt (Kosher or sea salt is best)

$^1/_2$ tsp pepper

Grapeseed, sunflower, safflower, or canola oil for frying

 SUPPLIES:

2 large bowls

measuring cups/spoons

spoons to mix ingredients

skillet (cast iron would be best)

slotted spoon

paper towels for draining

 PREPARATION:

Remove the seeds and finely chop the tomatoes.

Grate the zucchini.

Grate the onion.

Heat $^3/_4$ inch of oil in skillet over medium-high heat.

DIRECTIONS:

Combine the flour, baking powder and 1 tsp salt in a bowl. Set aside.

Combine the remaining ingredients except oil in another bowl. Add enough of the flour mixture to make a thick batter. Start with 1 $^1/_2$ cups and slowly add the rest. The amount of flour mixture needed is going to depend upon the liquid in the vegetables.

Heat $^1/_2$ to $^3/_4$ inch of oil in a nonstick frying pan. When the oil is hot, drop the batter by tablespoonfuls into the oil and fry until browned. Turn once to brown on both sides.

Remove with a slotted spoon and drain on paper towels.

YIELD:

serves 4 to 6

NUTRITION:

Nutrition Facts	
Serving Size 98 g	
Amount Per Serving	
Calories 83	Calories from Fat 3
	% Daily Value*
Total Fat 0.4g	1%
Cholesterol 0mg	0%
Sodium 175mg	7%
Total Carbohydrates 17.6g	6%
Dietary Fiber 1.9g	7%
Sugars 1.8g	
Protein 2.8g	
Vitamin A 11% •	Vitamin C 30%
Calcium 5% •	Iron 13%
* Based on a 2000 calorie diet	

Very low in saturated fat

No cholesterol

High in iron

High in manganese

High in phosphorus

High in potassium

High in selenium

High in thiamin

High in vitamin A

Very high in vitamin B6

Very high in vitamin C

NOTES:

In Greek: pronounced doh-mah-to-kef-TEH-thes

HURRY-UP HUSH PUPPIES

"Hush puppies" date back to the War Between the States, when soldiers would toss fried cornbread balls to quell barking dogs. It's also said that fishermen would create a batter out of the cornmeal that they used to fry fish, fry it in the fish oil, and give that to their dogs to eat. Whatever the original etymology, I LOVE hush puppies with fish dinners.

INGREDIENTS:

2 cups flour (I use fresh ground soft white)

1 cup corn meal (I use fresh ground organic popcorn)

1 tsp salt (Kosher or Sea salt is best)

2 tsp aluminum-free baking powder

$^{1}/_{2}$ tsp garlic powder

$^{1}/_{2}$ cup finely chopped green onions

1 egg

$^{1}/_{2}$ cup organic creamed corn

$^{1}/_{2}$ cup whole milk

oil for frying

SUPPLIES:

bowl

measuring cup/spoons

sharp knife and cutting board

frying pan

PREPARATION:

Finely chop green onion.

For the best tasting results, make this immediately after frying fish and use the same oil.

Otherwise, put 2 inches extra virgin olive oil in a deep frying pan or dutch-oven and heat to 375° degrees F (190° degrees C).

DIRECTIONS:

Mix together dry ingredients. Add the remaining ingredients and mix well.

Drop by rounded tablespoon into hot oil.

Cook until browned on one side, then carefully turn over and cook the other side.

Drain on paper towels.

YIELD:

About 20 hush puppies.

NUTRITION:

Nutrition Facts

Serving Size 94 g

Amount Per Serving	
Calories 206	Calories from Fat 18
	% Daily Value*
Total Fat 2.0g	3%
Saturated Fat 0.5g	3%
Cholesterol 22mg	7%
Sodium 353mg	15%
Total Carbohydrates 42.1g	14%
Dietary Fiber 2.7g	11%
Sugars 1.6g	
Protein 6.3g	

Vitamin A 4%	•	Vitamin C 3%
Calcium 8%	•	Iron 13%

* Based on a 2000 calorie diet

Low in sugar

High in calcium

High in iron

High in dietary fiber

NOTES:

I use grapeseed oil for deep frying.

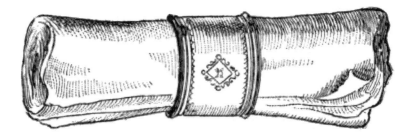

MEXICAN DOUGHNUT STRIPS (CHURROS)

This is my family's traditional breakfast for Christmas morning. It's a very light dough, crispy, with a delicate sweet flavor brought about by sprinkling it with sugar and cinnamon. I only make them for Christmas so that we have something special to look forward to every year.

 INGREDIENTS:

For the CHURRO:

1 cup water

$\frac{1}{4}$ cup unsalted butter

1 TBS sugar

$\frac{1}{4}$ tsp salt (Kosher or sea salt is best)

2 eggs

Canola or coconut oil for frying

1 cup flour (I use fresh ground soft white wheat)

For the DUSTING:

1 tsp cinnamon

$\frac{1}{2}$ cup sugar

NOTE: Alternately, drizzle with honey

 SUPPLIES:

heavy 2-quart pot

wooden spoon

cookie sheets

waxed paper

pastry bag with large star tip

heavy frying pan

paper towels

slotted spoon

 PREPARATION:

Line cookie sheets with waxed paper.

Mix $\frac{1}{2}$ cup sugar with cinnamon.

 DIRECTIONS:

Bring water, butter, sugar, and salt to a boil. Add the flour. Stir vigorously with a wooden spoon until the mixture forms a ball that doesn't separate. Cool for 10 minutes.

Add the eggs, 1 at a time, and beat with wooden spoon until smooth.

Spoon dough into pastry bag fitted with a large star tip. Pipe the dough into strips 2 to 3 inches long onto waxed paper lined cookie sheet.

Freeze strips about 20 minutes or until firm. (You can freeze them overnight as well).

While the strips are in the freezer, heat the oil to 375° degrees F (190° degrees C).

Drop the strips into the oil, a few at a time. Fry for 3 to 4 minutes or until browned.

Remove from oil with slotted spoon and put on paper towel lined plate.

Immediately sprinkle with sugar/cinnamon mixture.

 YIELD:

24 strips

 NUTRITION:

Nutrition Facts

Serving Size 94 g

Amount Per Serving	
Calories 194	Calories from Fat 84
	% Daily Value*
Total Fat 9.3g	14%
Saturated Fat 5.3g	27%
Trans Fat 0.0g	
Cholesterol 75mg	25%
Sodium 174mg	7%
Total Carbohydrates 24.1g	8%
Dietary Fiber 0.8g	3%
Sugars 7.6g	
Protein 4.1g	

Vitamin A 6%	•	Vitamin C 0%
Calcium 2%	•	Iron 7%

Nutrition Grade C+
* Based on a 2000 calorie diet

High in selenium

No Trans Fats

 NOTES:

You could also drizzle with pure or local raw honey.

SOPAPILLAS

Sopapilla means "little pillow" and can be used in a savory dish much like a tortilla or a pita bread. For this dish, I used them as a breakfast bread and drizzled them with honey. They were beyond amazing. A wonderful breakfast to kick of a *Cinco de Mayo* celebration.

 INGREDIENTS:

2 cups flour (I used fresh ground soft white wheat)

1 tsp aluminum-free baking powder

$^1/_2$ tsp salt (Kosher or sea salt is best)

2 TBS extra virgin coconut oil

$^3/_4$ cup warm water

extra virgin coconut oil for frying

honey (Pure, raw, local honey is always best) to drizzle

 SUPPLIES:

bowl

measuring cups/spoons

pastry cutter or fork

rolling pin

pizza cutter or sharp knife

frying pan

 PREPARATION:

Put enough coconut oil in your pan so that you will have about an inch of oil. Heat to just over medium heat

 DIRECTIONS:

Mix flour, baking powder, and salt. Cut in coconut oil until the mixture resembles fine crumbs. Stir in water. Let rest for about 10 minutes.

Put onto lightly floured surface and roll to about $^1/_4$ inch thick.

Using a pizza cutter or a sharp knife, cut into squares.

Gently slide a couple of pieces at a time into the hot oil.

Cook until browned (about 2 minutes.) The dough will puff up. Gently turn over and cook an additional minute or until the other side is browned.

Remove from oil and drain on paper towels.

Drizzle with honey.

YIELD:

About 12 pieces.

NUTRITION:

Nutrition Facts

Serving Size 464 g

Amount Per Serving	
Calories 1,164	Calories from Fat 271
	% Daily Value*
Total Fat 30.1g	46%
Saturated Fat 25.0g	125%
Cholesterol 0mg	0%
Sodium 1178mg	49%
Total Carbohydrates 193.8g	65%
Dietary Fiber 6.9g	27%
Sugars 1.4g	
Protein 25.8g	
Vitamin A 0% •	Vitamin C 0%
Calcium 26% •	Iron 67%
* Based on a 2000 calorie diet	

No cholesterol

Very low in sugar

High in selenium

High in thiamin

NOTES:

Try mixing a tsp of chili powder and a dash of cumin and sprinkle with that mixture for a more savory flavor.

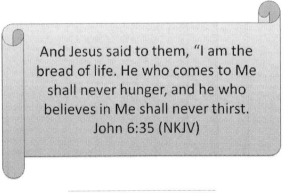

And Jesus said to them, "I am the bread of life. He who comes to Me shall never hunger, and he who believes in Me shall never thirst.
John 6:35 (NKJV)

ORANGE DROP DOUGHNUTS

I discovered this recipe when I had doughnuts on the menu one morning but had forgotten to set any yeast doughnut dough to rise. This is a quick and easy, sweet breakfast food that your family will love.

 INGREDIENTS:

2 eggs

$^1/_2$ cup sugar

2 TBS extra virgin coconut oil

2 cups flour (I use fresh ground soft white wheat)

2 tsp aluminum-free baking powder

$^1/_4$ tsp salt (Kosher or sea salt is best)

2 TBS orange zest (grated orange rind)

$^1/_2$ cup fresh squeezed orange juice

extra virgin coconut oil for frying

 SUPPLIES:

zester

juicer

bowl

wooden spoon

frying pan

 PREPARATION:

Juice the oranges.

NOTE: Depending on size, there isn't $^1/_2$ cup orange juice in just 1 orange. I only had 1 orange to spare when I first made this recipe, so I squeezed it yielding about $^2/_3$ cup and added orange juice from a carton in my fridge until I had $^1/_2$ cup.

Fill a frying pan with oil. You want at least an inch of oil in the pan. Heat it to 375° degrees F (190° degrees C).

DIRECTIONS:

Beat the eggs. Beat in sugar and coconut oil.

Sift together the dry ingredients.

Mix together the orange juice and orange rind.

Add the dry ingredients to the egg mixture alternately with the orange juice. Stir just until moistened.

Drop by spoonfuls into the hot oil. The dough will drop down, then rise to the surface as it cooks. When it's brown on one side, gently flip over and brown the other side. Remove from the oil with a slotted spoon and drain.

Sprinkle with powdered sugar.

Enjoy!

YIELD:

About a dozen doughnuts.

NUTRITION:

Nutrition Facts

Serving Size 102 g

Amount Per Serving

Calories 291	Calories from Fat 59
	% Daily Value*
Total Fat 6.5g	10%
Saturated Fat 4.6g	23%
Cholesterol 55mg	18%
Sodium 120mg	5%
Total Carbohydrates 52.0g	17%
Dietary Fiber 1.4g	6%
Sugars 18.6g	
Protein 6.3g	

Vitamin A 2%	•	Vitamin C 22%
Calcium 9%	•	Iron 13%

* Based on a 2000 calorie diet

Low in sodium

High in selenium

No Trans Fats

NOTES:

You can glaze these instead of sprinkling with sugar. Add $1/8$ cup boiling water to 1 cup powdered sugar and mix well. Dip the warm doughnut into the glaze.

APPLE FRITTERS

I made these for breakfast one Sunday morning, and my kids asked for them all week long. They were incredibly easy to make and tasted amazing. They are now a regular on my menu.

INGREDIENTS:

1 ¼ cup whole wheat flour (I use fresh-ground soft white wheat)

⅓ cup sugar

1 tsp aluminum-free baking powder

¼ tsp Kosher salt

1 ½ tsp ground cinnamon

¼ tsp nutmeg

½ tsp vanilla extract

1 TBS unsalted butter

1 egg

⅓ cup whole milk

1 ½ cups chopped apple

1 cup powdered sugar

2 TBS whole milk

oil for frying (I use grapeseed oil, extra virgin coconut oil, or organic canola oil)

SUPPLIES:

Large bowl & spoon

Measuring cups/spoons

Sharp knife/cutting board

Deep skillet

Slotted spoon

Paper towel lined plate

Small bowl & spoon

Wire rack

PREPARATION:

Fill skillet with about 1-inch oil. Heat oil in skillet to 375° degrees F (190° C)

Peel and chop the apples.

Melt the butter.

DIRECTIONS:

Mix the powdered sugar and the 2 TBS milk in a small bowl. Set aside.

Mix the dry ingredients in the large bowl. Make a well in the center. Add the milk, egg, melted butter, and vanilla. Stir until just mixed (do not use a whisk – the dough is really thick). Gently stir in the apples. (There is going to seem as much apples as there is dough – this is a good thing).

Test the oil by dropping a single water drop into the oil. If it skitters on the top, it's ready.

Place a spoonful of the batter in the oil (about the size of a golf ball). Add spoonfuls until you have 4 or 5 fritters in the oil. Don't overcrowd the oil.

Let cook for about a minute. Using the slotted spoon, carefully turn the fritters, and let them cook 45 to 60 seconds more.

Using the slotted spoon, carefully remove the fritters to the paper towel.

After a minute or two, roll each fritter in the icing you prepared.

Place on the wire rack to cool and dry.

YIELD:

about 16 fritters – about 8 servings

NUTRITION:

Nutrition Facts

Serving Size 86 g

Amount Per Serving	
Calories 204	Calories from Fat 24
	% Daily Value*
Total Fat 2.7g	4%
Saturated Fat 1.4g	7%
Trans Fat 0.0g	
Cholesterol 26mg	9%
Sodium 99mg	4%
Total Carbohydrates 42.4g	14%
Dietary Fiber 1.3g	5%
Sugars 26.0g	
Protein 3.2g	

Vitamin A 2%	•	Vitamin C 2%
Calcium 6%	•	Iron 6%

* Based on a 2000 calorie diet

Low in sodium

NOTES:

I use apples from my apple tree and typically make this while they're in season. Good apples to buy for this are Granny Smith or Fuji apples.

MUCH ADO ABOUT BREAD

Now that you've baked the recipes in this book, you've baked bread or made bread dough and yummy corn breads. You are probably wondering about some fun things to do with these recipes now. You have bread dough in the freezer? What can you do with it?

In this section, you'll find all sorts of fun recipes – from French Bread to Travel Sandwiches to Mini Quiche and many other delicious ideas.

FAMILY FAVORITE FRENCH TOAST

French toast is one of my favorite breakfasts.

I love having French Bread in my weekly menu, because that allows me to put French toast somewhere in my breakfast menu. I also love that this is another recipe my children can help me prepare.

 INGREDIENTS:

8 thick slices of French Bread (or any kind of bread – try it with Scrumptious Cinnamon Swirl Bread or Honey Oatmeal Bread.)

2 eggs

1 cup whole milk

1 TBS sugar

$^1/_2$ tsp ground cinnamon

$^1/_4$ tsp nutmeg (fresh ground with a zester is incredible)

$^1/_4$ tsp salt (Kosher or sea salt is best)

unsalted butter to taste

powdered sugar to taste

 SUPPLIES:

cutting board

bread knife

bowl

whisk

measuring cups/spoons

griddle or frying pan

spatula

 PREPARATION:

Slice bread in thick slices.

DIRECTIONS:

Whisk 2 eggs until well beaten. Add milk. Add spices and sugar. Mix well.

Heat griddle to about 375° degrees F. Melt butter on griddle.

Place bread in bowl and let soak for about 10 seconds. Flip over and let soak for at least 5 more seconds.

Put on griddle. Cook until browned (about 3 minutes – gently lift the edge of the bread to check.) Turn over and cook until the other side is browned.

Dust with powdered sugar.

YIELD:

4 servings

NUTRITION:

Nutrition Facts

Serving Size 38 g

Amount Per Serving	
Calories 67	Calories from Fat 12
	% Daily Value*
Total Fat 1.4g	2%
Saturated Fat 0.6g	3%
Trans Fat 0.0g	
Cholesterol 22mg	7%
Sodium 153mg	6%
Total Carbohydrates 10.6g	4%
Sugars 2.0g	
Protein 3.1g	
Vitamin A 1% •	Vitamin C 0%
Calcium 3% •	Iron 4%
* Based on a 2000 calorie diet	

High in selenium

NOTES:

You can use regular bread for this recipe – you don't need to use French Bread.

If you are feeling really decadent, you can use Banana Bread. That is SO amazing.

STUFFED FRENCH TOAST

I overheard someone say that they use their George Foreman grill to make pannini sandwiches. I immediately thought about using mine to make stuffed French toast. One morning, I tried it, and it was amazing – and so easy!

Slice a banana in half in the middle, then cut the remaining halves into three lengthwise slices.

Using whole wheat French Bread, prepare Family Favorite French Toast.

Dip bread into mixture. Only coating only one side.

Place slice on the heated grill egg side down. Add 3 slices of the banana.

Dip another piece of bread into the egg mixture, only wetting one side, and place on top of the banana, egg side up.

Place on your George Foreman grill. Close the lid and cook for 2 minutes.

Make sure you have something to catch the egg mixture that will be squeezed out of the bread from the weight of the grill lid.

After 2 minutes, turn over and grill for 2 minutes more.

Dust with powdered sugar.

EGG-IN-A-HOLE

This is one of my all time favorite breakfasts. I love fried eggs cooked medium, and I love soaking up the yolk with toast. This meal just puts it all together for me. The kids love it because it's "fun".

Start by slicing a nice, thick slice of bread.

Cut a hole out of the middle of it with a small biscuit cutter.

Butter both sides of the bread.

Heat a skillet to medium-medium-high heat. When the skillet is hot, put the buttered bread in it.

Place another tab of butter in the hole.

Gently crack your egg and slowly pour it in the hole. The slower you go, the more the egg is going to cook right there in the hole and be contained by the bread.

Monitor your bread. When the down side is browned, use a spatula and gently flip the whole thing over.

Cook until the bread is browned on the other side. The egg will be cooked medium – hard whites, soft yolks.

Brown the spare pieces in the same pan.

Serve and enjoy.

SAVORY CORNBREAD DRESSING

Until I made this recipe, I had never made any kind of stuffing or dressing before, other than pre-made stuff.

Working at the soup kitchen, I had seen the head cook there make it a few times, so I consulted her on how to make it on a scaled-down version. I was really pleased with the results.

 INGREDIENTS:

2 cups turkey broth (if you don't have any pre-made, you can use the juice from roasting your turkey)

1 recipe Old Fashioned Cornbread (see page 62)

about 8 slices whole wheat bread

1 medium onion

3 stalks celery

$^1/_4$ cup unsalted butter

1 to 2 TBS dried sage (depending on your taste)

2 TBS dried parsley

1 tsp salt (Kosher or sea salt is best)

$^1/_2$ tsp fresh ground black pepper

 SUPPLIES:

skillet   bread knife
wooden spoon   cutting board
bowl   measuring cups/spoons
13x9x2 baking pan -OR- ice cream scoop and baking sheet

 PREPARATION:

Prepare Old Fashioned Cornbread. Let cool.

Dice onion and celery.

Heat oven to 375° degrees F (190° degrees C).

Cube bread slices.

DIRECTIONS:

Melt butter in skillet over medium heat. Add celery and onion. Cook, stirring frequently, until soft.

Place bread cubes in large bowl. Crumble cornbread into the bowl. Mix well. Add seasonings and spices. Add onion and celery. Add turkey broth. Mix until moistened.

Spread evenly in 13x9 pan bake at 375° degrees F (190° degrees C) for about 25 to 30 minutes, or until the top starts to brown.

—ng an ice cream scooper, scoop out individual servings of the dressing and place them on a lightly greased cookie sheet. Bake at 375° degrees F (190° degrees C) for 20 to 25 minutes, or until browned.

YIELD:

8 servings

NUTRITION:

Nutrition Facts

Serving Size 100 g

Amount Per Serving	
Calories 145	Calories from Fat 44
	% Daily Value*
Total Fat 4.9g	8%
Saturated Fat 2.5g	13%
Trans Fat 0.1g	
Cholesterol 30mg	10%
Sodium 527mg	22%
Total Carbohydrates 21.0g	7%
Dietary Fiber 2.0g	8%
Sugars 3.3g	
Protein 4.9g	
Vitamin A 4% •	Vitamin C 2%
Calcium 9% •	Iron 7%
* Based on a 2000 calorie diet	

Low in sugar

Very high in antioxidants

NOTES:

You can put in a 13x9 pan if you didn't want to make individual scoops. Bake for about 30 minutes or until it starts to brown.

HALLEE'S FABULOUS 'TRAVEL' SANDWICHES

These sandwiches were initially inspired by a technique I observed on a Food Network show many years ago. We have perfected them for our family over the years. They are beyond delicious, incredibly good for you, and better the longer they sit. I promise you this. Make this sandwich just once with fresh, homemade ingredients and you will have discovered your very favorite sandwich.

There are so many variations, too. Try them "Vegetarian" or with any combination of toppings.

My family calls these "travel sandwiches" because whenever we go on a long road trip, we always have some in our cooler. Then when we stop for lunch, we just cut chunks of sandwich off and pass them out. Heaven.

 INGREDIENTS:

FOR EACH SANDWICH YOU NEED:

1 "quarter" loaf of French Bread

2 slices deli style turkey (or chicken or duck) breast luncheon meat*

2 slices deli style roast beef (or lamb or venison) luncheon meat*

3 slices Provolone cheese (or thin sliced Cheddar, Pepper Jack, or Swiss)

2 large Romaine leaves

2 tsp stone ground (or yellow) mustard

1 TBS Balsamic vinegar

1 TBS extra virgin olive oil

$1/2$ tsp Kosher or sea salt (NOT "iodized" table salt)

$1/4$ tsp fresh ground black pepper

Kosher dill pickle slices (to taste)

tomato slices (to taste)

onion slices (Purple, red, white or yellow to taste. We like purple on these sandwiches)

green bell pepper slices (or red or yellow to taste)

About 20 Kalamata olives, chopped —OR— 1 TBS Kalamata olive tapenade

OPTIONAL TOPPINGS IN QUANTITIES TO PERSONAL TASTE:

alfalfa sprouts

baby spinach leaves

shredded carrot

thin sliced celery

artichoke hearts

fresh cucumber slices

fresh zucchini slices

grilled eggplant slices

various green or black olive slices

fresh parsley

fresh dill

fresh cilantro

mushrooms

banana pepper/ pepperoncini / jalapeno slices

pimentos

feta or blue cheese crumbles

hard boiled egg slices

turkey bacon or beef bacon slices

SUPPLIES:

food processor or whisk and bowl

sharp knife & cutting board

measuring cups/spoons

plastic wrap

mandolin (optional)

PREPARATION:

Prepare French Bread, breaking the dough into four smaller loaves instead of two.

Slice your vegetables.

I like my sub veggies to be sliced thin, so I use a mandolin for consistent even slices. Some high end food processors also have nice slicer attachments. A circular meat slicer is also an option.

DIRECTIONS:

Cut a wedge out from the top of the bread.

Line the bread with your cheese slices.

Top with the meat.

Top with the onion.

Add green pepper.

Top with the olives.

Add tomato.

Add any other additional optional toppings to taste.

In a small bowl (or a food processor if you are making a large batch), whisk together mustard, vinegar, salt, pepper. Continue whisking as you slowly add the oil, forming an emulsified dressing. If you are using a food processor, it should create a milky suspension of all ingredients.

Drizzle the dressing over tomatoes.

Top with Romaine lettuce leaves:

Replace the top of the bread:

Now for the secret to these sandwiches. **WRAP IT UP TIGHT!**

Wrap it just as tightly as you can with plastic wrap.

Now, stick it in the refrigerator for at least two or three hours. The longer it sits, the more that emulsified dressing is going to marinate into the olives, marry with the onions and peppers, and just make the entire sandwich the most fantastic flavor combination your mouth has ever experienced.

YIELD:

1 loaf will serve 2 (unless feeding a teenager, in which case 1 loaf serves 1)

NUTRITION:

Nutrition Facts	
Serving Size 96 g	
Amount Per Serving	
Calories 228	Calories from Fat 97
	% Daily Value*
Total Fat 10.8g	17%
Saturated Fat 5.8g	29%
Trans Fat 0.0g	
Cholesterol 22mg	7%
Sodium 439mg	18%
Total Carbohydrates 21.5g	7%
Dietary Fiber 0.7g	3%
Sugars 6.9g	
Protein 11.0g	
Vitamin A 2% •	Vitamin C 3%
Calcium 7% •	Iron 25%
* Based on a 2000 calorie diet	

Very high in vitamin B6

Very high in vitamin B12

High in iron

Very low in cholesterol

Low in sugar

NOTES:

For beef, lamb, venison and the like, I will often season and sear a good sized roast then pop it in the rotisserie oven for a few hours. Once it cools, it goes through the circular meat slicer and I end up with very thin sliced perfectly cooked sandwich meat.

For turkey, duck, or chicken I will do much the same. I will either oven roast it, crockpot cook it, or let it go in the rotisserie oven. I can put the breast on the circular meat slicer for some really good thinly sliced deli style luncheon meat.

If I don't have any of my own homemade meat on hand, I am careful to choose a brand with neither preservatives nor nitrates.

PEACHY OVERNIGHT FRENCH TOAST

I made this to take to church for breakfast for my Sunday School class. It was really good, and required no syrup for serving. I made it the evening before, popped it into the oven 30 minutes before we had to leave for church, and was able to serve it still warm to my class.

 INGREDIENTS:

10 or 12 slices of homemade bread (I used homemade whole wheat French Bread for one pan and homemade Honey Oatmeal Bread for the other pan. It's hard to say which pan was better. They both tasted pretty amazing.)

1 cup brown sugar

$\frac{1}{2}$ cup unsalted butter

2 TBS water

1 quart peaches (I used home canned – store bought peaches will usually be in a 29-ounce can)

5 eggs

1 TBS vanilla extract

ground cinnamon

 SUPPLIES:

bread knife and cutting board

saucepan

small bowl and whisk

13x9 baking pan

tinfoil

 PREPARATION:

Slice the bread $\frac{3}{4}$ inch thick.

Roughly chop the peaches.

 DIRECTIONS:

Put the brown sugar, butter, and water in saucepan. Bring to a boil. Reduce heat to low and simmer for 10 minutes. Pour into the bottom of your baking pan and tilt the pan around to spread the syrup.

Sprinkle peaches evenly over the syrup. Top with slices of bread.

In a small bowl, whisk the eggs and vanilla. Pour evenly over the top of the bread.

Cover with tinfoil and refrigerate overnight.

The next morning, remove it from the refrigerator at least 30 minutes before putting it in the oven.

Preheat oven to 350° degrees F (120° degrees C).

Remove the foil and bake, uncovered, for 30 minutes. The toast will start to brown.

YIELD:

12 servings.

NUTRITION:

Nutrition Facts	
Serving Size 99 g	
Amount Per Serving	
Calories 193	Calories from Fat 69
	% Daily Value*
Total Fat 7.7g	12%
Saturated Fat 4.2g	21%
Trans Fat 0.0g	
Cholesterol 66mg	22%
Sodium 219mg	9%
Total Carbohydrates 26.7g	9%
Dietary Fiber 1.2g	5%
Sugars 13.2g	
Protein 5.0g	
Vitamin A 8% •	Vitamin C 5%
Calcium 3% •	Iron 7%
* Based on a 2000 calorie diet	

High in vitamin A

High in vitamin C

NOTES:

Try this with canned apples or pears in place of the peaches and you will be equally successful and pleased with the result.

BEEF BACON QUICHE TARTS

This is the perfect brunch dish. The beef bacon and the onion and peppers really enhance the flavor of the eggs.

I used the Granny Everman's Yeast Roll recipe using fresh ground flour to make the crust.

Before my family stopped eating pork, I have sampled quiche dishes made with traditional pancetta and also with good old pork bacon. I use beef bacon which is so much better than pork bacon. It is richer, thicker, less greasy and more savory. You could substitute turkey bacon in this dish but I chose not to because I was concerned it might be too chewy. Beef bacon is crispy.

This dish was a huge hit when I took them to church for breakfast for my Sunday School class.

INGREDIENTS:

About one-third of Granny Everman's Yeast Roll recipe

2 eggs

$^1/_2$ cup shredded sharp cheddar cheese

6 ounces cream cheese

5 tsp whole milk

1 TBS finely chopped onion

5 beef bacon strips (uncured is best)

SUPPLIES:

frying pan or skillet

mixer and bowl

measuring cups/spoons

muffin pan

plate lined with paper towels

PREPARATION:

Prepare the Granny Everman's Yeast Roll recipe. (See NOTES.) If you're using pre-frozen method, bring the dough to room temperature.

Chop beef bacon into small pieces and fry or fry then chop into small pieces.

Drain on paper towels.

Preheat oven to 375° degrees F (190° degrees C).

Lightly grease muffin tin with a paper towel dipped in butter.

DIRECTIONS:

Beat cream cheese and milk until smooth. Add eggs. Add onions, peppers, and cheese. Mix well.

Pinch a piece of dough about the size of a ping pong ball. Work it with your fingers until it's flat. (You can roll it flat, but that seemed like excessive work to me).

Line the muffin tin. Place bacon crumbles in the bottom of the crust.

Pour in the egg mixture.

Sprinkle top with bacon pieces.

Bake for 8 to 12 minutes or until set (a knife inserted in center will come out clean.)

Serve warm.

YIELD:

8 cute little quiche tarts

NUTRITION:

Nutrition Facts

Serving Size 50 g

Amount Per Serving	
Calories 131	Calories from Fat 66
	% Daily Value*
Total Fat 7.3g	11%
Saturated Fat 3.8g	19%
Trans Fat 0.0g	
Cholesterol 52mg	17%
Sodium 172mg	7%
Total Carbohydrates 6.5g	2%
Sugars 1.4g	
Protein 6.0g	

Vitamin A 4%	•	Vitamin C 0%
Calcium 4%	•	Iron 4%

* Based on a 2000 calorie diet

High in protein

High in iron

NOTES:

When you make the Granny Everman's Yeast Roll recipe, save a portion in the freezer. After it rises the first time and you punch down the dough, break off however much you want to save. Put it in a freezer bag, make sure you remove all of the air, and label it "yeast roll dough" so you know what it is. It will safely keep for up to six months.

Then you won't have to make a recipe that takes 2 hours to rise the morning you want to serve these Beef Bacon Quiche Tarts. The night before you're going to make this recipe, remove the dough from the freezer and pop it into the refrigerator to thaw. Remove it from the refrigerator in the morning and allow it to come to room temperature while you are doing the remainder of your prep work for this recipe.

Once it has reached room temperature, just follow the remainder of the instructions in the Granny Everman's Yeast Roll recipe that happen after the first rise and you will have a scrumptious crust for your quiche.

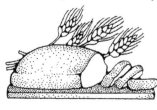

AFTERWORD

By Hallee the Homemaker

FROM WALKING DEATH TO ETERNAL LIFE

There is an popular cultural phenomenon that has shambled into our entertainment in that last several years – zombies. They've dragged their way into bookstores, movie theaters – even my 4-year-old when driving through the Kentucky woods one night said, "We're in the zombie forest!"

We have gone from werewolves and vampires to a zombie apocalypse. Just how did these decomposing, flesh-eating creatures end up "front and center" everywhere we turn? And, just curious, why are they so hungry if they're dead? Dead things don't require nourishment! They can't possibly digest anything or put those nutrients to use. The whole notion is just silly. The bottom line question is this: what is this obsession with the walking dead?

The message of this cookbook is threefold. First, I wanted to share really fabulous recipes with you and your families. It is my most earnest prayer that these recipes will be your "go to" bread recipes – as they are for me – and that you will share them with your family, friends, and future generations.

Second, I wanted to help illustrate the difference between what are commonly referred to as "flour" and "bread" in our modern world and what real bread and real, whole grain flour is. The cover of this book illustrates a lone survivor heading toward rich, real, whole grain fresh bread while leaving the dead commercial white bread in his wake.

White flour contains only one third of the grain and is almost nutritionally void. It is put through a minimum of twenty industrial processes in order to have a nearly indefinite shelf life. Back when white flour was first introduced, people who ate it actually sickened and died in a very short span of time. In order not to lose market share, producers had to add back in "vitamins" in the form of industrial grade chemicals and now this nearly non-food is legally labeled "enriched" because they remove the hundreds of naturally occurring vital nutrients found in whole grain flour and reintroduce two or three, thus "enriching" it with enough nutritional value that you don't die when you eat it.

Eating modern white bread and using white flour exclusively can contribute to obesity, heart disease, high blood pressure, diabetes, and worse. It is worth your time and effort to invest in a grain mill and fresh grains and … believe me … you will never understand how amazing bread made from fresh milled flour can taste until you feel it melt in your mouth.

There is a third and final message I wanted to convey and it is this.

Human beings are obsessed with death as a whole, and throughout history, always have been. I think of Mary Shelley's *Frankenstein's Monster* or the macabre works of Edgar Allen Poe, or Michael Jackson's *Thriller* video, or the *Night of the Living Dead* movies. Zombies are not a new idea.

Writers and producers throughout our modern history, and even before, have used a dead and zombified theme to present their message, whether that message is deeply spiritual and a lesson about "playing god" or something fun and fluffy to market a bubblegum musical score and sell records.

In his letter to the church at Ephesus, the apostle Paul writes:

> "And you He made alive, who were dead in trespasses and sins, in which you once walked according to the course of this world, according to the prince of the power of the air, the spirit who now works in the sons of disobedience, among whom also we all once conducted ourselves in the lusts of our flesh, fulfilling the desires of the flesh and of the mind, and were by nature children of wrath, just as the others." Ephesians 2:1-3 (NKJV)

In essence, Paul compared a pre-Christ life to someone walking around, dead inside. This is not talking about a physical death, but a spiritual dead. We once were *The Walking Dead*. All of us. We were suffering and in pain, moaning, constantly craving unsavory things.

The beautiful thing is that Paul doesn't stop there. He goes on to say:

> "But God, who is rich in mercy, because of His great love with which He loved us, even when we were dead in trespasses, made us alive together with Christ (by grace you have been saved), and raised us up together, and made us sit together in the heavenly places in Christ Jesus, that in the ages to come He might show the exceeding riches of His grace in His kindness toward us in Christ Jesus" v.4-7

That's right. Even though we were once walking around dead inside like zombies, God loved us so much that He brought us back to life again through his only begotten son, Christ our Lord. Our spirits are given life the moment we repent of our old life and accept Christ into our hearts and into our new lives. Because of God's amazing grace, we can know what it is like to be fully alive inside and no longer dead.

Christ said he did not come to only give us life but to bring us more abundant life. Imagine that! Not only do we have more abundant life here on this earth, but we also have a promise of eternal life in the very presence of our Creator.

It is my sincere prayer that if you do not know Christ that you come to know Him before this life is over.

MEASUREMENTS & CONVERSIONS

Liquid (Volume) Measurements (Approximate)				
1/3 TBS	1/6 fl oz	1 tsp	5 cc	5 ml
1 TBS	1/2 fl oz	3 tsp	15 cc	15 ml
2 TBS	1 fl oz	1/8 cup	6 tsp	30 ml
1/4 cup	2 fl oz	4 TBS	12 tsp	59 ml
1/3 cup	2 2/3 fl oz	5 TBS & 1 tsp	16 tsp	79 ml
1/2 cup	4 fl oz	8 TBS	24 tsp	118 ml
2/3 cup	5 1/3 fl oz	10 TBS & 2 tsp	32 tsp	158 ml
3/4 cup	6 fl oz	12 TBS	36 tsp	177 ml
7/8 cup	7 fl oz	14 TBS	42 tsp	207 ml
1 cup	8 fl oz	1/2 pt	16 TBS	237 ml
1 pt	16 fl oz	1 pt	32 TBS	473 ml
2 cups	16 fl oz	1 pt	32 TBS	473 ml
2 pts	32 fl oz	1 qt	1/4 gal	946 ml 0.946 l
4 cups	32 fl oz	1 qt	1/4 gal	946 ml
8 pts	1 gal/128 fl oz	4 qts	1 gal	3785 ml 3.78 l
4 qts	1 gal/128 fl oz	8 pts	1 gal	3785 ml 3.78 l
1 l	1.057 qts			1000 ml
1 gal	qts	128 fl oz		3785 ml 3.78 l

Dry (Weight) Measurements (approx)		
1 oz		30 g (28.35 g)
2 oz		55 g
3 oz		85 g
4 oz	1/4 lbs	125 g
8 oz	1/2 lbs	240 g
12 oz	3/4 lbs	375 g
16 oz	1 lbs	454 g
32 oz	2 lbs	907 g
1/4 lbs	4 oz	125 g
1/2 lbs	8 oz	240 g
3/4 lbs	12 oz	375 g
1 lbs	16 oz	454 g
2 lbs	32 oz	907 g
1 k	2.2 lbs/ 35.2 oz	1000 g

(DRY)		
	1 pt	0.551 l
	1 qt	1.101 l
	1 peck	8.81 l
	1 bushel	35.25 l

(WEIGHT)		
	1 oz	28.35 g
	1 lbs	453.59 g
	1 lbs	0.454 kg

(LENGTH)		
	1 in	25.4 ml
	1 in	2.54 cm
	1 ft	304.8 ml
	1 ft	30.48 cm
	1 yd	914.4 ml
	1 yd	91.44 cm

ABOUT THE AUTHOR

HALLEE BRIDGEMAN is a best-selling Christian author who writes action-packed romantic suspense focusing on true to life characters facing real world problems. Her work has been described as everything from refreshing to heart-stopping exciting.

An Army brat turned Floridian, Hallee finally settled in central Kentucky with her family so she could enjoy the beautiful changing seasons. She enjoys the roller- coaster ride thrills that life with a National Guard husband, a teenage daughter, and two elementary age sons delivers.

When not penning novels, she blogs about all things cooking and homemaking at Hallee the Homemaker™ (www.halleethehomemaker.com). Her passion for cooking spurred her to launch a whole food, real food "Parody" cookbook series. In addition to nutritious, Biblically grounded recipes, readers will find that each cookbook also confronts some controversial aspect of secular pop culture.

Hallee loves coffee, campy action movies, and regular date nights with her husband. Above all else, she loves God with all her heart, soul, mind, and strength; has been redeemed by the blood of Christ; and relies on the presence of the Holy Spirit. She prays her work here on earth is a blessing to you and would love to hear from you. Contact information is on her website.

COOKBOOKS BY HALLEE:

Fifty Shades of Gravy, a Christian gets Saucy

The Walking Bread, the Bread Will Rise

Iron Skillet Man, the Stark Truth about Pepper and Pots

FICTION BOOKS BY HALLEE:

Sapphire Ice, book 1 of the Jewel Series

Greater Than Rubies (a novella inspired by the Jewel Series)

Emerald Fire, book 2 of the Jewel Series

Topaz Heat, book 3 of the Jewel Series

Christmas Diamond (a novella inspired by the Jewel Series)

A Melody for James, book 1 of the Song of Suspense Series

An Aria for Nicholas, book 2 of the Song of Suspense Series

A Carol for Kent, book 3 of the Song of Suspense Series (upcoming)

HALLEE ONLINE

Hallee Newsletter
http://tinyurl.com/HalleeNews/

Never miss updates about upcoming releases, book signings, personal appearances, or other events. Sign up for Hallee's monthly newsletter.

Hallee the Homemaker blog
www.halleethehomemaker.com/

Hallee Bridgeman, Novelist blog
www.bridgemanfamily.com/hallee/

HOUSE OF BREAD

Better known as Bethlehem of Judea, the old Hebrew name *bêth lehem*, meaning "House of Bread," is known as the birthplace of King David and, above all, of Our Lord, Yeshua, known as Jesus of Nazareth. Thus, the "House of Bread" that is Bethlehem brought forth the Bread of Life that is our Savior.

The House of Bread Books™ imprint is pleased to publish healthy nutritious information in the form of cookbooks or informational pamphlets in order to better serve our community – the human race. We publish to reach every tribe and every nation for God has made of one blood all nations of men.

We pray that you enjoyed this fun attempt to redeem a recent secular phenomenon. Mostly, we pray that you come to know the joy and peace that is in serving Our Lord and Savior who is the King of kings, Lord of lords, and the Bread of Life.

Send inquiries to:

HOUSE OF BREAD BOOKS™
an imprint of: Olivia Kimbrell Press™
PO Box 4393
Winchester, KY 40392-4393

Or e-mail admin@oliviakimbrellpress.com

FIFTY SHADES OF GRAVY

While confronting and redeeming a recent popular secular phenomenon, Hallee Bridgeman, A.K.A. "Hallee the Homemaker" rides the gravy train to triumph and hilarity with her premiere cookbook, revealing the secrets of the penultimate comfort food – gravy. Fifty Shades of Gravy "a Christian Gets Saucy!" is a cookbook wrapped in a parody surrounded by a comedy with a tongue firmly inserted into a cheek – but the recipes are deadly serious and may leave readers licking the gravy boat.

Her famous whole food, real food recipes bathe in luxuriant liquid comfort with recipes that are sure to captivate and enslave any audience.

Hallee starts with stocks and broths and then explores every shade of gravy you can whip up. Some recipes are entire meals and some are simple sauces while still others are gravies served alongside a traditional holiday feast.

There are meaty gravies, comfort food gravies, vegan gravies, gluten-free gravies, and even chocolate gravies! For any gravy question you were too ashamed to ask, this saucy Christian shares the answer.

Visit http://tinyurl.com/50gravyshades for more saucy information.

IRON SKILLET MAN

It's a bird! It's a plane! It's a cookbook!

Move over men of steel! Make room mutants, aliens, and chemically or radioactively enhanced rescuers! Prepare to assemble your spatulas and get your "Flame on!" while the heroic Hallee the Homemaker™ (whose secret identity is Christian author and blogger Hallee Bridgeman) swings into action and shows her mettle with her third title in the Hallee's Galley parody cookbook series.

Is your skillet-sense is starting to tingle? Don't start crawling the walls, worthy citizen. Hallee constructs comic fun, jabbing at the cultural obsession with super powered heroes and villains. Along the way, readers will thrill to action packed explanations, daring "do it yourself" techniques, tremendous tips, and lots of real food/whole food recipes that achieve truly heroic heights. Ironically, while just a mild mannered cookbook by day, wrapped in a parody and surrounded by a comedy by night — the recipes are absolutely real and within the grasp of ordinary beings. Along with revealing the stark truth about pepper and pots, learn how to clean and season cast iron and care for cookware so it will last for generations. Recipes run the gamut from red meats to vegetables and from fish to fowl. Super skillet breads and divine desserts rush to the rescue.

In these colorful pages, you might just discover the x-factor to overcome even the most sinister kitchen confrontation. With Iron Skillet Man fighting for you, ordinary meals transform into extraordinary super powered provisions, whether cooking over a campfire or a conventional stove top.

Visit http://tinyurl.com/ironskilletman for more slices of information.

INDEX

cocoa powder, 71

coconut milk, 65, 66

Colby, 26

corn husks, 94, 95, 97

corn masa flour, 90

corn meal, 6, 107

cornbread, 4, 73, 75, 76, 94, 107, 123, 124

cornmeal, 6, 15, 16, 17, 18, 73, 75, 76, 83, 84, 85, 97, 107

cracker, 83, 84, 85

crackers, 83, 84, 85

cranberries, 86, 87

cream cheese, 71, 72, 131, 132

creamed corn, 107

CRUSTY CHEESE BREAD, 24

cumin, 94, 112

D

Daniel fast, 45, 83, 105

DELICIOUS CRANBERRY NUT BREAD, 86

dietary fiber, 91, 108

Dirty Dozen, 6

doughnut, 109, 113, 114

doughnuts, 113, 114

E

EASY CHEESEY CHILI EMPTANADITAS, 98

EGG-IN-A-HOLE, 122

H

luncheon meat, 125, 128

M

MA-MAW LUCILLE'S BUTTERMILK BISCUITS, 60

manganese, 51, 68, 106

maple syrup, 49, 53, 55, 57, 58, 67, 68

MARVELOUS MAPLE MUFFINS, 67

Masa Harina, 94, 97

Measurements & Conversions, 136

MEXICAN DOUGHNUT STRIPS (CHURROS), 109

milk, 5

mint, 104, 105

molasses, 53, 57, 61, 71, 72

Mozzerella, 26

MUCH ADO ABOUT BREAD, 118

muffin tin, 34, 67, 69, 71, 132

muffins, 4, 67, 68, 69, 70, 71, 72, 73

N

niacin, 91, 96

nitrates, 128

Numbers, 3

nutmeg, 54, 56, 71, 115, 119

O

OATMEAL, 4, 8, 49, 119, 129

oatmeal, 4, 8, 49, 119, 129

oats, 4, 9, 49, 50, 58, 70

preservatives, 128

protein, 133

Proverbs, 8

provolone cheese, 24, 25, 26, 125

Psalms, 3

PULL APART YEAST, 34

pumpkin, 54, 55, 71, 72

Q

quiche, 118, 131, 133

QUICK BREADS, 48

QUICK CINNAMON ROLLS, 62

R

raisins, 27, 29, 48, 64, 65, 66

riboflavin, 91

roast beef, 125

rolls, 18, 31, 32, 34, 36, 62

S

sage, 123

sandwich, 12, 125, 128

sandwich, 125, 128

saturated fat, 16, 19, 22, 32, 42, 44, 79, 89, 91, 93, 103, 106

SAVORY CORNBREAD DRESSING, 123

scones, 48, 65, 66

SCRUMPTIOUS CINNAMON, 27

V

W

3-16

DISCARD

Made in the USA
Charleston, SC
10 March 2016